DELiGHT

DISRUPT

DELIVER

GROW YOUR BUSINESS USING THE POWER OF SMALL SURPRISES

DELIGHT
DISRUPT
DELIVER

GROW YOUR BUSINESS USING THE POWER OF SMALL SURPRISES

MILTON COLLINS

First published in 2021 by Dean Publishing
PO Box 119
Mt. Macedon, Victoria, 3441
Australia
deanpublishing.com

DEAN PUBLISHING

Cataloguing-in-Publication Data
National Library of Australia
Title: Delight Disrupt Deliver: Grow Your Business Using the Power of Small Surprises
Edition: 1st edn
ISBN: 978-1-925452-25-9
Category: BUSINESS/Entrepreneurship

The views and opinions expressed in this book are those of the author and do not
necessarily reflect the official policy or position of any other agency, publisher,
organization, employer or company. Assumptions made in the analysis are not reflective
of the position of any entity other than the author(s) — and, these views are always
subject to change, revision, and rethinking at any time.

The author, publisher or organizations are not to be held responsible for misuse, reuse,
recycled and cited and/or uncited copies of content within this book by others.

In loving memory of my mother,
who supported and
believed in me and gave me
every encouragement to succeed.

To my children, Emma and Lachie,
of whom I am so proud, and
for whose benefit I want to succeed.

Milton is sharing more in his
INTERACTIVE book.

See exclusive downloads, videos,
audios and photos.

DOWNLOAD it now at
deanpublishing.com/smallsurprises

CONTENTS

FOREWORD

BRAD SUGARS

Many business books on the market today over-promise and complicate what it takes to build a prosperous and enduring business. Without the right knowledge and mentorship, few business owners build the fundamentals well enough to grow and soon get trapped in the vicious cycle of working harder, not smarter.

When I started ActionCOACH® in 1993, I knew success required finding and developing reputable, world-class coaches that could help business owners grow and transform their businesses. Milton Collins is such a coach. His reputation for success is well-established; not only has Milton built some of Melbourne's most iconic businesses, but through ActionCOACH® he has helped other business owners grow exponentially and see their profit, purpose and passion rise.

During my early years in the business sector, my mentor Jim Rohn taught me something very valuable; in fact, it's one of the most powerful insights anyone could ever learn in business. It's this:

Business is all about people.

The great leaders don't underestimate the power of this statement. Don't be fooled by its simplicity. People are at the core of everything. They make or break your business.

Delight. Disrupt. Deliver: Grow Your Business Using the Power of Small Surprises is built around this core principle and gives people practical ways to disrupt their industry and over-deliver in wonderful and surprising ways.

Milton started his working days on a family farm in regional Victoria, and I believe this helped mould the great business coach we see today — a man who has never forgotten about small, family-owned businesses, or the community at large. In today's changing business environment, business owners need someone who has 'been there and done that', someone who knows how to generate income and build a sustainable business that lasts. Now more than ever, business owners need real tools and strategies that work.

I have often said if you build the team, they build your business, and this book truly reiterates that statement. It helps business owners gain focus, build team unity and apply extraordinary customer service practices.

I encourage readers to apply these formulas and take advantage of the wisdom offered. These lessons are timeless. They don't go out of fashion and they are proven. They are disruptors. But as I warned earlier, don't be fooled by the simplicity — mastery happens in the execution of them. You must ACT on these great principles. Execution sets you up for success.

Brad Sugars
Founder and CEO of ActionCOACH®

INTRODUCTION

In his famous Commencement speech at Stanford University, Steve Jobs said, "You can't connect the dots looking forward; you can only connect them looking backwards. So you have to trust that the dots will somehow connect in your future."

Looking back at my own life, I can see he was right. I didn't know that growing successful businesses would be 'my thing', but connecting the dots backwards, I can see it was always there.

I grew up on our family farm—beef cattle and wheat—and I knew the value of an honest day's work—early mornings, carting hay, cutting thistles, irrigating, cattle mustering, drenching and marking, and loads of other chores.

It was an idyllic lifestyle: swimming in the river, channels and dams, shooting, horse riding, having a large range of vehicles to learn to drive, loads of space and places to explore. We showed stud cattle, competed in horse shows and I started a local riding group which became the local pony club in our area.

My mum and dad were very different from each other and in many ways, they both shaped my future decisions with or without my consent.

My father was a workaholic with a quick temper, he was violent to mum and us kids. He was always blaming us for things going wrong — it was our fault if the cattle broke away while we were helping, even though we did our best. But it was also our fault if we were not there to help. We could not win and there was no motivation to succeed — just fear.

I had no respect for him at a very early age and decided I wasn't going to be anything like him. He treated people and animals with cruelty and I swore I'd never treat people or animals like he did.

Despite my young age, and the fact I was frightened of him, I stood up to him to try and protect my mother. To cope — I shut off and got on with things. In those days, domestic violence wasn't a topic of conversation, although we lived in this situation, we didn't speak about it, nor did we think the police would do anything about it. In fact, one night a friend and I rushed to the police station to get help for my mother, and when they turned up, they did not do anything. Not-a-single-thing! I didn't speak about it to anyone. My mother, brothers and I found our own ways to cope.

My mother's way of coping was her own, she became a leader in the community. She was the first local cub leader, President of the Country Women's Association, Sunday School teacher at our local church and became President of the School Council and parents group. Her way of coping was to get on with things and become an involved leader within the community.

So, I unconsciously inherited her leadership strengths and simultaneously realised the type of man I wanted to become. Or more so, who I didn't want to be like.

I was the eldest child of three boys, our youngest brother was born with a mental disability. We always treated him the same, but between dad's violence and my brother's disability — the pressure weighed heavily on my heart.

In many ways, boarding school became my refuge. I was away from the pressures of home, but a strange sort of guilt hovered over me knowing that my mum and brothers were still on the farm with Dad. I often worried about how they were coping.

I went to a conservative boarding school, The Geelong College, even from my early school days, I was a people-orientated young man. I wasn't a sportsman. I was never good at sport, and had no interest until I started playing hockey at school. But I loved horse riding. That was a real passion for me. I wasn't naturally skilled, I was really scared at times and always aware of the danger. Over time, I found ways to overcome the fear and went eagerly into the most dangerous equestrian sport — Three Day Eventing — dressage, steeple-chase, roads and tracks, jumping over big cross-country fences and show jumping.

When it came to career options, both my mother and the school encouraged me to go to university. I wanted to explore a career in hotel management although I hadn't done any waiting due to boarding school, I'd always loved parties and people. Whilst researching career options, I fell in love with the idea of hotel management. In that era, there weren't many study options in Australia. I researched a fabulous hospitality and management university in Lucerne, Switzerland, and realised that was where I wanted to go. I was excited about this possibility and figured that I could work part-time to pay for it, hopefully with a little bit of support from my parents too.

But my parents and school advisor said, "No, you don't want to be a hotel manager, it's not a real career." They wanted me to get a degree. But that passion for management was always there. Instead I did 'the right thing' — an economics accounting degree at The Australian National University. I found it quite dry and didn't like it as much as hospitality. But as I was committed, I made sure I finished my degree (but had a great time as well). I also worked in hospitality and taught horse riding — my two real passions.

In those days, all the major accounting firms came out to campus to interview students. And we were encouraged to go along, even just for the interview practise, if nothing else. I got offered five jobs from five different accounting firms, the highest number out of all my friends. Interestingly, I was offered that, not because of my marks, but because during the time I was studying, I was teaching horse riding and became the Chief Instructor of an equestrian centre. I realised that the employers were far more interested in what I was doing outside my studies. They loved the fact I had developed some people and business skills.

They asked me why I chose accounting. They could see my passion for people outweighed my passion for numbers. Of course, they were happy that I had an economics degree, but it was the people-

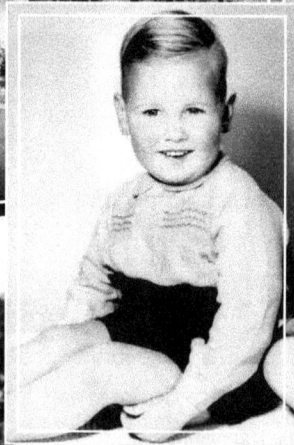

orientation that secured my first job at PriceWaterhouse Coopers, more so than just my academic performance.

The business man inside of me was emerging with every new skill I built inside and outside the workplace.

On the home front, after completing my Economics degree at age 22, I moved my mother and disabled brother out of that awful situation whilst my middle brother Ian stayed on the farm. It was a major moment for all of us, a new beginning. Ian was more interested in his own future and never ever helped in any way. He was much more like my father. So it left me to support and look after my mother and disabled brother. It was time to take our power back and make our own rules. It was time to get on and make the most of our lives. I was supporting my mother and brother while my father contested the family settlement for over 10 years.

I was working as an accountant at PriceWaterhouse Coopers (PwC) and throughout my adult life worked my way through a number of positions. During this time I was very busy with my horse riding competitions and wanted to return to the country so that I could combine horse riding with a professional career. After much searching, I found a very progressive firm in the country that was to become the RGM Financial Group where I was offered a partnership at 26 years of age. I left the group after 15 years and started my own firm which became Collins Ryan. I grew this firm rapidly and then sold it to a publicly-listed company, Stockford Ltd in 2001. Unfortunately, Stockford went into liquidation and I was only partially paid for my shares.

Interestingly, my passion for hospitality management hadn't wavered and it was time to do something about it. My professional life was wonderful and my skillset was strong. So I purchased a run-down conference centre and turned it into an iconic Country House Hotel and Conference Centre. It took some work but the ride was worth it. We won many awards including Telstra Business of The Year in the Macedon Ranges and were selected for case studies in Excellence by Victorian Tourism. During this time I sat on many boards and committees.

I realised that creating iconic places is something I loved to do and excelled at. So in 2015, I was appointed the Chief Executive Officer of Transport Hotel in Melbourne's Federation Square, including Taxi

Kitchen Restaurant, Transport Hotel, Transit Roof Top Bar and Taxi Riverside Events.

I was hired to rebrand and market the businesses, and to improve the culture and profitability. I managed the strategic operation of the business as a destination event space. It was about making this hub a thriving and cosmopolitan go-to venue for people. Creating a spark and electricity that made it unique and profitable.

It was a tough gig made harder by undermining long-term personnel. Of course, behind the scenes of success there is always a lot of blood, sweat and tears. A lot of mistakes and problems, but this is what business does. It helps create your character. It reveals strengths and weaknesses.

And now, as a business coach, I can see the personal journey is just as transformative as the business journey. It's inevitable that growing a successful business will develop your character, it will reveal strengths and weaknesses, it will challenge you. And if done with a growth mindset and willingness to learn, it will turn you into a leader of integrity.

Helping people build their own successful business is why I get up and do what I do every day. It lights me up. If I can help people not only build great businesses but develop life-long traits like leadership, community spirit and caring for people — then I'm living the full dream. And guess what? I am.

But no one could have told me when I was a young child that the lessons I learned and the traits I inherited, were part of the greater plan. As Jobs said, connecting the dots backwards, it all makes sense.

Reflecting back at my own life I can see that the fundamentals to success were already present: treating people well, giving people a great experience, finance, hospitality, community, growing businesses. It was all there throughout my entire life but bringing them all together, learning along the way, and never giving up was the formula that created success.

Now, I feel it's time to give back, to share the ways that really helped me grow and sustain successful businesses. Although I certainly don't hold all the answers, I love to share the ones that I know made the biggest differences. And the funny thing is, the littlest things made the biggest differences.

Throughout this book you will see that I built iconic businesses, often from the ground up, based around a whole lot of little things.

Sure, the vision was big but it was the small things done well that really escalated into big success. Simply through making a whole lot of small consistent wins in the right direction, your business can boom like never before.

This may not be your typical business book, in fact, I hope it's not. Typically, business books focus on overhauling large elements, KPIs or motivating staff. Although I believe in those things as well, from my experience the greatest growth and most sustainable and accessible changes are done in little and surprising ways.

In other words, **growing a business is all about the little things because those little things become big things.**

So, if you want the big things, begin with the little things.

Milton Collins

PART ONE

BUSINESS FOUNDATIONS

*"Don't work for recognition —
do work worthy of recognition."*

Jackson Brown Junior

THE POWER AND THE PROBLEMS WITH FIRST IMPRESSIONS

As the saying goes, "You never get a second chance to make a first impression." There are many things you can repeat in life, and in doing so, can expect to get better results. Making a first impression isn't one of them.

First impressions last — and once made, a first impression can go one of two ways: in your favour or against you. If it's not a favourable first impression, you may never get the chance to rectify it.

Research indicates that it takes anywhere between five and 15 seconds to form a first impression about someone.[1] The current rule-of-thumb seems to settle somewhere around seven seconds.

That's a very swift (and lasting) 'first' impression. Many times, a first impression remains a 'forever' impression and can be almost impossible to overcome.

In a way, it's not fair that mere seconds or even milliseconds can make or break the fact that someone will or won't do business with you. But if you know the rules, then you know how to play the game.

And whether you agree with the rules or not, it helps to know them, right? The better you know the rules, the better you play the game and the more you win.

So it makes sense in any business meeting or relationship to make a good first impression. Get it right from the get-go. Don't set yourself up to lose. Those first few seconds of meeting someone or someone arriving at your premises, you can't repeat. You never get them back. Make them count.

From my experience, the way you start a relationship is the way it continues. It's very rare and extremely difficult to turn a bad impression around. So take the lead and get it right the first time.

SIMPLE WAYS TO MAKE A LASTING FIRST IMPRESSION

Don't be fooled into thinking that you're already making a good first impression. There are always ways to improve.

There are five keys ways to make a good first impression so you can Delight, Disrupt and Deliver in your key industry. These are:

#1. SMILE ☺

#2. SYSTEMS ⚙

#3. SCRIPTS 📄

#4. SERVICE 🤝

#5. SURPRISES 🎁

Perhaps you're already doing four out of five, but adding the fifth element of 'surprise' can be the difference between being good and being memorable. Anyone can be good but only great businesses are memorable. These five keys will help your first impression be outstanding.

#1. SMILE

SMILE FOR A FEW SECONDS

Don't be afraid to go back to basics, to start with the timeless simplicity of a genuine smile. If it takes seconds to make a good impression, why not fill it up with three things:

1. A greeting
2. Their name
3. A smile

"Hello, Catherine, my name is Milton. It's wonderful to meet you." It's not hard to say these things, but it sounds so much better when there's a smile in your voice and on your face.

Sure, it's basic but it's also deliberate and engaging.

Using someone's name is music to their ears, it instantly personalises the greeting and helps them know that they aren't a number, they are a person and you are happy to see them. Yes, we are all human and everyone likes to feel comfortable and cared for.

Smiling has also been shown to be a psychological sign of altruism. As you will discover throughout this book, altruism is the key to a memorable business. In fact, it makes your business stand out.

When you smile at someone, in this case, Catherine, it makes her more likely to like and trust you. It makes you seem more approachable and caring. Flashing a genuine smile means so much more than curving your mouth and showing your pearly whites — a genuine smile is one of the most beautiful sights in the world. If you and your team members aren't smiling, you're doing business all wrong. Whatever business you're in — you're in the smiling business. Okay, maybe not funeral directors, but you get my point.

A smile transcends language barriers instantly and is shown to reduce stress in the workplace. Research shows that a genuine smiling face creates customer joy and enhances brand appeal. Notice, I said *genuine*. I'm not talking about encouraging cheesy, fake smiles, people can pick superficial care very easily. I'm talking about a welcoming and caring attitude. But in saying that, any smile — even if it is a little forced, is better than none.

It's no surprise that we see billboards and ads with smiling people (not including the fashion industry trend of keeping a straight and morbid expression down the runway). In general, most photos on your website should also be of you and your team looking happy.

2016 research from Cornwell University[2] proved this theory correct. Professor of psychology, Vivian Zayas and her colleagues found that people continued to be influenced by another person's appearance even after interacting with them face-to-face. They found that seeing a photo of someone (even after they had met) predicted how they felt about them for one to six-months after their interaction.

So your presentation in photos and on your website should also be looked at as a first impression — because they are. As are your social media pages and your LinkedIn profile. Everything really is a first and lasting impression.

"A smile is the universal welcome."

— *Max Eastman*

AVOID FAST-TALKING

So many companies I've helped over the years answer the phone by rattling off their company name like they're reciting the alphabet; there's no deliberate engagement or smiling tones. It's said like a fact more than a greeting. No one likes this. The only place people like fast-talkers are at auctions or long-winded speech ceremonies, and the latter is in hope of them finishing quick.

Yes, be deliberate in your tone. I am. I ask my team to take a breath and smile BEFORE they pick up the phone. The tone of a smiling person is undeniably warm. Attitude begins *before* you walk into work, *before* you pick up the phone, *before* you say "hello". Your tone and your attitude speak more loudly than what you actually say.

One recent scientific study showed that people made obvious and somewhat accurate impressions from a voice. The study showed a simple "hello" was enough to elicit an impression simply based on a vocal tone.[3] The researchers write that "perceived vocal personality influences mate selection, leader election, and consumer choices."[4]

Encourage your team to use genuine, warm and smiling vocal tones.

GIVE YOUR NAME

Personalise it. Tell them who you are. Always give your name. Then ask, "How may I help you?" Or something softer to understand what their query might be. People want to know who they're talking to.

Let's be honest, people get bombarded with marketing calls all too often, they hate it. The noise in the background, a person from the other side of the world asking them personal questions in two-seconds flat. No one likes that type of call.

Be different to the norm. Really listen to people. Give your name. Tell them that you'll help them and follow through. These simple things speak volumes. It makes their day easier for them, not harder.

You may be thinking, that's so obvious Milton, our company already does this. Great! I hope so. Doing it is great, not doing it is catastrophic.

ALWAYS USE THEIR NAME

Always use someone's name. Whether on the phone or in person, using a person's name is another way of saying, "You're important". It's deeply personal and shows warmth and understanding and care. It makes them your number one priority and gives your attention to them.

Ask how they like to be addressed and use their name like that every time you see them. Write their name down, put it in your work system. If a person's name is James but he prefers to be called Jim, call him Jim.

He prefers it. It doesn't matter if his licence or passport says James, he likes Jim more. Then Jim it is.

A study published in *Brain Research* showed that our brains light up when we hear our own name.[5] Interestingly, the study showed this 'brain ignition' didn't happen when we hear other people's names, only our own. The brain scans clearly showed obvious activation and activity when someone heard their name.

Of course this doesn't mean that you repeat their name incessantly, that would be a bit of overkill and possibly lead to feelings of suspicion. But don't underestimate the pure music someone's name is to their ears.

IGNORANCE IS NOT BLISS

Of course, a warm greeting isn't always possible, sometimes receptionists are busy on the phone or talking to a customer. However, how many times have you been ignored because someone is busy? It happens way too often.

There is nothing worse than walking into a place and being ignored. Actually, there is — team members chatting amongst themselves about their weekend social life *and* ignoring you. I've often seen that in retail outlets and even professional practices where they're not customer-focused.

Being casual and conversational has its place, but ignoring a customer so you can share your personal stories with another team member is a huge no-no.

It's important that the whole team understands if the reception is busy then anyone on the team (including the director, CEO or partners) answers the phone or attends to the client. Implement a rule from the beginning that everyone gets acknowledged and that isn't one person's job — it's everyone's job.

These things are simple but the question is: **are these simple things implemented?**

And that's why systems are important.

#2. SYSTEMS

Many business owners believe they already have systems because they have a computer system. They're great but systems are for every process not just what happens on a computer system or your database.

Systems are the backbone to optimal functionality.

I'm a great believer in systems. You need to have good systems in place so that your team, and even you, have something reliable to lean on. A trusted and secure system to fall back on can make the difference between being mediocre or being memorable. You can't ways remember everyone's name for example, but you can ensure it's in the system and accessible to everyone on the team immediately.

So when you're in a meeting, whether it's on the phone or in-person, you have a trusted system in place. And by a trusted system, I mean one that is **practised and implemented**. One that everyone is trained in and feels at ease in using.

I encourage team members to keep records of our customers special likes and dislikes, this is not to be a snoop, but so we can all cater to *their* individual needs and not have to ask them the same questions every time we meet. They don't want to have the same conversation over and over again with every staff member. They want to know that we listen, that we know them, that we understand them.

I believe in systems for:
- How to greet people
- How to handle a complaint
- How to answer the phone
- What to say to a difficult client
- How to ensure the place is clean and tidy
- How to communicate with team members
- How to ensure clients are happy
- How to begin and continue relationships

The list goes on. In short, I believe in systems for all important business processes.

Some people may say, "Milton surely you don't need a system for the obvious things like smiling to clients or not ignoring them?" Yes, you do. You need to set the rules of the game so your team knows them. If you don't have the foundations right you can't build. If you have the systems right, you can relax in knowing that it's been taken care of and you can go and focus on building the business.

Here is a simple example of a system.

MOVE TO MEET PEOPLE

When someone comes into the reception, our system is to step out from behind the reception desk to greet them. That's more special than staying put. It's obvious to stay behind the counter, it's a barrier. That barrier is not warm. If you can, get out from behind your desk and go out and welcome them, and say, "Hello Bob, Great to meet you. Have a seat and Milton will be with you shortly."

Your physical presence reflects — 'you're important, you matter'.

If they have an appointment, you should know their name *before* they enter, or have a damn good guess by the time they arrive. If they're an ongoing client, you should definitely know their name. Because it's in the system. Yes, systems are there to help you, not just be a to-do list.

Getting up and out of your seat is a simple exercise, but the small act of effort makes a huge difference. It's also good for your health too. Sitting down for too long creates stagnation. Get out of the desk and move around.

So, if you're training staff, begin with the greeting.

Train your team in the art of making other people feel good.

This type of training is often overlooked or not given precedence over computer skills or record-keeping. It's the most important system you can begin with. It helps people know what to do and helps you repeat first impressions.

If you're busy doing other things and you're caught off guard, it's easy to fall back into the system if you know it. You can just fall back into the standard routine. By all means, try to improve it, of course but at least you've got that structure, you have a minimum requirement.

A system is the minimal requirement. If you can better it, that's fantastic. Go for it. Grow and develop your systems — but don't forget to implement the basics before you go for so-called sophistication.

I must admit, my basics are pretty high, they're not too basic but they are formulated around extreme customer service. That's the secret many forget — your systems are designed around your core philosophy — your unique-selling-point — which in this case, is customer experience. Yes, systems are in place to serve your customers and give them a great experience and give your business the optimal chance for success. Systems means you do it deliberately — every day, every time.

Think about some systems you can implement today that will make your business more customer-focused. I'm sure you can list three immediately:

1. ....

2. ....

3. ....

Now, I'm an ActionCOACH®, so it's natural that I'm going to ask you to take action right now and implement your 3 systems.

Yes, it's only the first chapter of this book, but this book is for action and understanding, not just to read. If you use this book in this way, you *will* grow your business!

Using the power of small surprises gives you big results. As the late businesswoman, Anita Roddick said, "If you think you're too small to have an impact, try going to bed with a mosquito."

#3. SCRIPTS

To make systems work, it's important to use scripts. These aren't just for movie actors, they are to help people feel at ease with the interactions that inevitably pop up in business. Why not arm your staff with conversational ammunition and armour?

As I said earlier, often I'll hear a receptionist rattle off the company name so quickly because they're doing it all day, I get that, but they either mumble it or rush it. This is really insinuating to the client, *I'm in such a hurry* and the client gets the impression that your company is too busy to deal with them. Scripts are powerful because they don't leave first impressions to chance.

Scripts help your team convey a warm, inviting presence every time. It's critical. The first person they interact with can decide if they do business with your company or not. If your receptionist is having a bad day, the script can save them and help ease the tension of the day.

Scripts aren't supposed to be recitations, they supposed to take pressure off staff and give them guidance. It's really a form of branding; a way to ensure a good customer experience. Scripts aren't just for the phone but for all greetings, and for answering FAQs.

You'll be surprised how many people just want the simple things: manners, courtesy, a door opened for them. These things aren't hard but sadly they're becoming rare.

SCRIPTS NEEDS TO BE PRACTISED

Role play your scripts with your team and make it fun and engaging. It sets the culture and shows them 'this is how we treat people'. We care. We make effort. This is who we are.

I encourage lots of role-playing. Get your team members to offer examples of what they've used successfully or something else that's really impressed a customer. Mindset matters and your team's involvement is critical to your business. Most times, your staff are the ones at the coalface, saying the hellos, doing the phone calls, handling the complaints. Equip them with scripts so they don't have to face the problems unarmed. That's your duty as a leader.

Scripts help everyone. They're not supposed to be rehearsed lines that sound repetitive or like a soap-opera rerun — but make them fun, engaging and dynamic. Give them zest and allow room for personality. That's what scripts are — a framework with space for adding some charisma, some personality and personal touches.

Language is important. Use language that supports your clients and makes them feel comfortable and welcomed.

Now, I'm not talking about over-the-top language filled with superlatives, that may come across as false and cheesy. I'm saying positive but authentic, warm and engaging language. Scripts provide a balanced framework for language.

SCRIPT YOURSELF FOR SUCCESS

Before I started my CEO position with Taxi Group, I met with all the team leaders, the management, and the senior managers because Taxi included four different businesses — Transit Rooftop Bar, Transport Hotel, Taxi Kitchen and the soon to be redeveloped Taxi Riverside at Federation Square.

I asked to speak to all the leaders. I thought it was important that they got to meet me personally and understand more about me and what I believe in. But more importantly, I wanted to meet them personally and get to know them. Many of them were nervous. So was I actually.

I spent quite a bit of time writing my own script. I scripted what I wanted to say and how I wanted to say it. It was an important talk and I didn't want to leave it to chance. I wanted to let them know how I operated. That our culture was an open-door policy and that I loved feedback. I scripted a section about being open to their opinions and ensuring they felt part of the business too. I asked them what issues they thought we needed to improve on, and if they were on-board with a new vision and future.

Through this script, they got to see my enthusiasm for the business and that I was interested in making it work for all of us. This began a great dialogue and through this open-style meeting I learned that they had never had a team meeting. The managers from each department had never met regularly although they were in the same building. Not once had they met to speak about strategies or sharing ideas.

That was the first step, to make sure there were weekly team meetings, not only within their own team, but also with each of the managers and the assistant managers from each department. And this all started with a mindful script. A deliberate script that was really about deliberately building a new culture and forming a new way of doing things.

Scripts give you the chance to communicate in the way you want. Scripts aren't just for the front desk receptionists, they can be used across a diverse and broad range of business practises, from CEOs to managers and all team members.

Can you think of 3 areas in your business that could improve with a well-built script? Is it in meetings, on the phone, with quotes, with staff?

1. ....

2. ....

3. ....

What would you say? How would you say it?

....

....

....

....

....

....

#4. SERVICE

There's a universal saying: "Treat others how you would like to be treated." Or "Do unto others as you would like them to do unto you." It sounds nice, but I suggest that you DO NOT follow that advice. That's right, don't follow this old adage if you want to get very successful.

This method basically suggests that if you give people want you want or need then everything works out great. I suggest this instead:

Work out the way people want to be treated — and do that!

Let's say that again in another way:

Don't treat people the way you want to be treated,
treat them the way they want to be treated.

This will change your business very quickly. It's a subtle but potent power. Write it down and put it up in your office or workplace — yes, it's that imperative.

What you believe is great customer service may in fact be very annoying to your client. Let me give you an example. When I ran Campaspe House, some people arrived exhausted and just wanted to be left alone. They wanted to get to their room, go to sleep in a warm, clean, comfortable bed and think of nothing else until morning. We made that happen for them as swiftly and as easily as possible.

Others arrived full of beans looking for something fun and social. They wanted to know what they could do and where they could visit. They wanted chit-chat and details. They wanted directions and brochures. They wanted laughs and late meals. We made sure that happened.

Now, imagine we treated them based on what WE wanted not what THEY wanted. Imagine if we asked our exhausted client to do what we found helpful to us — fill out forms, take a tour of our hotel. They'd resist it and find their first experience with us annoying. Sure, we would get what we wanted but this would be stupid — because in doing so, we'd give our customer a very annoying first experience. Next time, they'd book a place where they didn't have to interact with staff.

Imagine if we treated our active, social customer like our exhausted client. They'd feel it was poor customer service.

You need to look deeper than the customer, deeper than the sale. You need to look at the person and see what they want. Read in-between the lines and deliver. That's the difference between good customer service and memorable customer service.

Some clients want to make fast decisions, some want to move slow. It's up to you to find out what they want, how they think, how they like to be treated, how they like to make decisions — and let them do that.

Service isn't just the "would you like fries with that?" method. That's upselling, it's about discovering what they like and who they are.

A research firm Greenfield Online and Datamonitor/Ovum analysts, measured the cost of poor customer service in the U.S. They discovered **that 71% of consumers have ended a relationship due to a poor customer service experience![6]**

And furthermore, the average customer ended 1.2 relationships per year due to poor service and 61% took their business to a competitor.[7] Ouch!

Yes, you can inadvertently make your competitors extremely successful if you fail in customer service. So, you not only make your business fail, you also make someone else's business grow exponentially.

As Bill Gates, founder of Microsoft said, "Every day we're saying, 'How can we keep this customer happy?' How can we get ahead in innovation by doing this, because if we don't, somebody else will."

But think of it the other way around too. What if your competitors aren't doing things and you are! This is where you can DISRUPT your industry, by doing things in a new way, things your competitors aren't doing.

Now, I can't help but wonder if some businesses from this study, believed they were giving great service but the customer didn't like the way they were being treated and therefore believed it was poor service. Perhaps they had different reference points on what constitutes 'good service'. Perhaps they were following the 'treating others how you would like to be treated' method instead of 'treating others the way THEY wanted to be treated' method.

We'll delve into this deeper later in this chapter.

THE COST OF POOR CUSTOMER SERVICE IS MORE EXPENSIVE THAN YOU THINK

A 2018 report called "Serial Switchers" by NewVoiceMedia showed that poor customer service is costing businesses more than $75 billion a year. That's an increase of $13 billion in two years since its previous report.[8] And that's only a US stat.

On a global scale, a Genesys report, with research firm Greenfield Online and Datamonitor/Ovum analysts indicated that more than $300 billion is lost each year worldwide due to bad customer service, and with that $243 billion is being spent with competing companies.[9]

We can all understand when people aren't happy, they may look elsewhere but what I really noticed in the Serial Switchers report was this:

- **86% of customers surveyed said that if there was an emotional connection with a customer service agent, they would be willing to continue to do business.**
- However, only 30 percent felt the companies they had interacted with during the past year had made that connection.

86% is a massive number of people wanting an emotional connection in business. In other words, MOST people, want an emotional connection in business.

But I'm not surprised because that has been my experience too. People want to feel connected to your business, your team, your vision. And what I'm advocating for here is that you don't do that by default. You do that through deliberate care and action. Giving people what they want (an emotional connection and good customer service) makes your business grow and thrive.

Dennis Fois, Former CEO of NewVoiceMedia said this, "In today's Age of the Customer, personal, emotive customer interactions play a critical role in bridging the gap for what disruption and digital innovation alone cannot solve. For brands to compete — and win — in CX in 2018 and beyond, service leaders must ensure their teams optimize processes and communication in ways that create positive emotional experiences for customers."[10]

So how do you create those positive emotional experiences? Through the element of surprise.

#5. SURPRISE!

Good business is not enough, you need to be memorable. You need to stand out from your competitors. Little things that can help you do that. The art of surprise. The Wow factor! Put the DELIGHT back into business.

Now, I'm not talking about sending a client a printed Christmas card with your logo all over it. Nor am I talking about the old boys' club ideas of having a semi-naked woman pop out of a birthday cake. Although you'd certainly be memorable, you'd be memorable for all the wrong reasons.

I'm talking about a real surprise — something they don't expect that absolutely DELIGHTS them. The word delight (C 1200 *delit*) means "that which gives great pleasure".[11]

So, how much pleasure are you bringing to your customers?

Many believe that providing good customer service is the wow factor, it's not! That's old school business. The new way of doing business is making it an experience.

Good customer service is a great basic ingredient — but it won't get you to rise beyond mediocre. Most people expect good customer service, they complain if they don't get it.

But what they remember is **Extreme Customer Service**. *The Delight Factor*. It's not about going the extra mile once, but going the extra miles always. And the extra mile should not be done is a way that seems bothersome, like it's a burden. It's a pleasure to serve, to please, to ensure people are feeling comfortable, satisfied and delighted.

Surprises don't have to be big statements. I'm not talking about being Oprah and surprising an entire room with a note under their seat and giving them a new car. Though you can if you want. I'm talking about intimate surprises, meaningful moments they're not expecting.

If you run a hotel for example and find out that your client loves tennis, buy the latest tennis magazine and put it on their bedside table with a little note. If you don't have a tennis court, tell them you can hire the local court on their behalf. Don't just give directions, make the call, and hire it for your guest.

A true surprise is doing the unexpected in a positive way. Neuroscientists tell us that a release of our feel-good chemicals dopamine and serotonin happen when we are surprised and these trigger the reward system in our brain and floods us with bursts of happiness.[12]

Mega US company, Zappos,[13] goes to great lengths so the customer's orders are received before they expect it. The "under-promise, over-deliver element". They use free express shipping and have a promise to "deliver WOW through service".

The brain buzzes when surprised. When the good but unexpected happens. Think of the kick you get when you score a car park right out the front of a busy restaurant when it's raining. Or the tiny unexpected delight when you receive a complimentary coffee and biscuit that you weren't expecting.

One study in *The Journal of Neuroscience*[14] showed the power of unpredictable small surprises. 25 adult volunteers underwent MRI scans while having fruit juice or water squirted into their mouths through a tube either in a predictable or unpredictable manner.

During the predictable run, water and juice alternated at fixed intervals of 10 seconds. During the unpredictable run, the order and intervals were random. The subjects were then asked which drink they preferred.

The brain scans showed that the brain's pleasure centre was most strongly activated when the squirts were unpredictable. And it didn't matter whether the subjects preferred juice or water. Associate professor of neuroscience at Baylor College of Medicine in Houston and co-author of the study, Dr. P. Read Montague said, "The region lights up like a Christmas tree on the MRI." He also suggests "people are designed to crave the unexpected."[15]

Now, if mere squirts of juice or water can achieve such a brain spark, imagine what unexpected brain-delights you can trigger in your customers.

Remember it's not in the predicable that you gain this Delight Factor. It's in the unexpected delight. Get used to looking for better ways to give people a better experience. Ask yourself, *is there something else we could do to achieve that extra level of awesome customer service? How can we delight our clients?*

Running a business is all about a lot of little things. Improving little things can make a big impression in the future. Constantly fine-tuning those little things can make your business great.

Always try to think of something your clients don't expect or do something over and above what they expect to be normal. And that's what will change your business. Little things are not usually expensive. It's easy to give away a free drink, but I don't think customers get delighted or remember that as well as some sort of extra service or extra caring factor.

**It's to give them something positive that
they don't expect that really works.**

DELIGHT FACTORS I CAN IMPLEMENT IN MY BUSINESS

It's time for a little brainstorm. Think of some ways you can DELIGHT your clients (but you have to make sure it's what they would like not what you would like).

....

....

....

....

....

....

You see, these little things are big! People dismiss little things and only focus on the big things. It's good to focus on the big things too but taking your eye off the little things can be detrimental.

To stick with my own 'surprise philosophy' here, I am giving you the reader a little surprise too.

FREE scripts! These are the scripts I personally use to nail a first impression. Begin them in your business and with your team TODAY.

★ How to answer the telephone right, every time
★ How to deal with customer complaints effectively

Head to **deanpublishing.com/smallsurprises**

BUSINESS FOUNDATIONS

CULTURE IS KING

Culture is a buzz word and it should be timeless.

The Cambridge dictionary defines workplace culture as "the beliefs and ideas that a company has and the way in which they affect how it does business and how its employees behave."[16]

So, here's what I think culture is: the vision, values, systems, attitudes and standards that contribute to a company's habits and behaviours. It's what we see and don't see. It's the vibe beyond branding.

Culture is more important than strategy. If you can get the right culture in the business, it makes a critical difference. To get the right culture, your team need to understand what your vision is and what your goals are. What the standards and behaviours are. And I mean *really* understand them.

When I'm hired to coach a business and first go to their premises, I'll ask the receptionist or someone in the team if they know what the vision of the business is. They never do. Never. I've never had one person tell me.

The best I've heard is, "Well, that's what's on my boss's wall." Or "I think we'll be talking about that in our next meeting."

There's no point having a vision or a goal in business if your team don't understand it. But understanding isn't enough, a lasting business vision and culture is to be lived.

Culture should support all people within it. It should always be inclusive and transparent. If you haven't defined your business vision and culture, then you should do it immediately.

A strong vision is the centre-point for all decisions, I encourage businesses to make their decisions in line with their vision. So, when you need to make a big or small decision you can ask: *Is this decision aligned with the vision of the business?*

Your vision and your decision-making criteria should be so aligned that when you or your team wonder — *should I do this or that?* They can immediately ask, *does this align with the vision?*

Here are some examples of great business visions:

- **Tesla:** To accelerate the world's transition to sustainable energy.
- **Microsoft (at its founding):** A computer on every desk and in every home.
- **ActionCOACH®:** World Abundance through Business Re-education.
- **TED:** Spread ideas.
- **IKEA:** To create a better everyday life for the many people. IKEA say that "Our business idea supports this vision...so [that] as many people as possible will be able to afford them".
- **My vision:** To create profitable businesses that run so well that your clients keep coming back, your staff want to work for you and you actually have a life outside your business.

See how the business vision drives decisions?

You want your team to feel part of the business, like it's their business too. They've got to feel ownership. They've got to be proud of it and be responsible for the business too. When you pay their wages, their livelihood depends on it and it's important that they take pride in their contribution and feel part of the greater vision. It's important that they look after the customers, that they grow the business, that they help make the business sustainable, so they're so proud of it. Essentially, they are growing the business too. They are essential to the vision.

Help them become customer-focused. Anything they do has got to be about the customer and the business will benefit from that. Look after your customers, look after your team, and they'll look after the business.

"Customer service shouldn't just be a department, it should be the entire company."

— *Tony Hsieh, Zappos*

ENVIRONMENT AND ATTITUDE

What does the environment of your business say about you?

I'm amazed at the number of premises with a dirty bin out the front or a car park full of rubbish. Be it the car park, or the entrance, if it's not clean, it's unimpressive.

Make sure you've got areas where people can park. If you don't have parking on site, make sure when people make an appointment, you reply with an email, "Welcome to (Insert Business Name) — here is some information about where you can park."

If you're in a city, for example. Even if they know the city well, it doesn't matter. You care enough to show that you'll make it easy for them. How many places when you make an appointment, give you advice on where you might be able to park? That sort of stuff, it's not rocket-science. It's easy. But often forgotten.

Better still, at Taxi Kitchen, we negotiated special discounts for our customers from local car parking facilities.

Simple things matter.

Pot plants outside a business, especially restaurants, can make a major difference. We always ensured that we had beautiful plants outside the front door, and they had to be really healthy and well-maintained. There's nothing worse than half-dead pot plants outside your premises. It's not Halloween.

Now, you don't have to have green thumbs to accomplish this. There's enough companies around where you can hire plants or pay someone to maintain them. Or there could be someone on your team who loves gardening. Just ask them. Then it's even better because they'll take more pride in the plants and check them as they go past every day.

We did this with one of our clients, a very high-profile gardener. We had a lovely garden section on the side of our office and I hired him to redesign it and plant it out. It looked spectacular. And it fulfilled many purposes. One, it was a really great impression when our clients arrived. It looked impressive. It wasn't just professional, all of a sudden there was an inviting and lovely garden with an outdoor sitting area. In good weather, we'd meet there with clients too. Also with the team, they had somewhere to go with lunch. It was a multi-purpose garden.

It also created an instant referral resource for the gardener. Clients would walk past and say, "Oh wow, who did your garden?" We'd hand over the business card of our client and in turn it gave us the opportunity to get referrals too.

> To receive a free referral strategy designed by Milton, please go to **deanpublishing.com/smallsurprises**

IS YOUR ENVIRONMENT SET FOR SUCCESS?

Everyone loves a nice environment. Beautiful, spacious and nurturing environments make us feel at ease and relaxed. Workplaces such as Google, Dropbox, Airbnb, Lego, Nokia and Facebook are notorious for their incredible workplaces. But not everybody is Google, right? But it's not all about the budget, it's about creating a pleasant and inviting environment.

Most people think about first impressions as appearance, more so than attitude. It's both. But a bad attitude makes any environment ugly. Environments are more than visual.

An environment can also mean resources for your team. Some companies don't value the simple things, or will spend money on fancy marketing before they update an old worn-out computer system.

2018 reports from J.Gold Associates LLC show that running an older computer system can make your employees up to 29% less productive. Not because of them but because they have to wait for the damn computer to catch up with them. According to Intel's website, every 5-year-old PC in your business could be costing you $17,000 a year in lost productivity.[17]

Now, of course, Intel is a computer company so it's in their best interest to show us these type of stats. But the point is not about upgrading computers but thinking about your overall environment. Is it set-up for success?

Is your business environment updated and ready for business? Does the working culture need an update?

**Environment in business means both the
internal and external environment.**

External — cleanliness, buildings, parking, signage, gardens, surroundings.
Internal — culture, vision, team, attitude, systems, practises, behaviour.

Internal and external factors represent your business. Some people only focus on looks, on the visual appeal but fail in delivering quality and implementing systems. Others have great systems but lack thinking about attitude or culture. I've seen many banks with state-of-the-art systems but with the personality of wet cardboard.

A great business understands that EVERYTHING in business represents your business.

Attitude is often overlooked, but it's critical. Personally, I hire people with the right attitude because I know I can help teach and train a person's skillset.

As Richard Branson said about his company Virgin, "We look for people who are friendly and considerate, and who like working with others. From our airlines to our call centres, and our office buildings to our gym floors, you will always see smiling people working together to get the job done. These personalities make our staff successful, and, in turn, our businesses successful. They also keep our company culture vibrant."[18] (We will discuss this in greater length in Part 2 — Team Foundations).

Yes, you need some basic skills depending on the role or profession, but attitude creates the environment and culture. People with the right attitude are the best, they look after your business and the customers. That's critical but it's only step one. Then you need to give them the tools, the systems, the scripts, the right equipment and information.

ECX — EXTREME CUSTOMER EXPERIENCE

When I talk to many of my clients and friends about what makes their business special, often they tell me it's their incredible customer service. But when I delve a bit deeper I find that they really don't understand how to deliver consistent customer-focused service. They don't know how important it is. Or, they think having satisfied customers constitutes 'good customer service'.

Think of extreme sports, they aren't your vanilla experience. They do flips and turns and all sorts of crazy things. Extreme customer service is your version of that, but in business. And you make it look effortless.

Jeff Bezos from Amazon says, "The best customer service is if the customer doesn't need to call you, doesn't need to talk to you. It just works."[19]

In all my businesses, we made sure that our attention to our customers was the **most critical part of the business.** Not third on the list — or if we were having a particularly good day — it always was priority.

Sure, we did some flips and tricks in an extreme way to make it happen. But that's your job — to make good things happen for your customer.

When we owned the Campaspe Country House, as part of the hospitality industry, we had a lot of competition. We purchased it as a rundown conference centre and strived for a point of difference. We chose it because of the location — it was close to the airport, it had easy access to Melbourne city, it was in a lovely rural regional environment setting and it had good local wine and food.

The place had its own character, but more importantly it was an emerging area. It wasn't high-profile like the popular areas of Daylesford, Mornington Peninsula or Yarra Valley, so we had to have a point of difference. We decided to couple its natural character and location with extreme customer service. We built an ethos that was all about focusing on our guests and simple processes were put in place from day one to ensure we always sought to improve and become more innovative. Always.

The Campaspe Country House homestead was located at the end of a beautiful tree lined driveway. From the reception, we could see guests arriving by car before they entered the main building. Because of this we made a rule that no guest was allowed to come in the door without someone opening the door and greeting them. We had plenty of warning because the driveway was long, but the rule became second nature because we all understood that was important. And it was always done.

Secondly, when the guests arrived, a description of them would be written down discreetly so that the whole team could refer to that person by their name. That information was collected during the day and all the night staff would know the guests and their names. It was a very powerful thing to visiting guests. The guests were blown-away when everyone in the team already knew their name before they had even met.

Extreme customer service never feels extreme — it feels wonderful. We would constantly sit down with the team and ask:

- "How do we impress these guests even more?"
- "What else can we do to make a difference?"
- "How can we care more?"
- "How can we give them a surprise?"

We always looked at what we did well and what we could do better next time. Sometimes guests would arrive in a bad mood, couples that had just had a fight or a business person whose flight was delayed. Our team would understand that some guests had a particularly challenging day but they didn't want to continue to feel bad. It's important to consider how people feel and adapt to what they need. Help them feel better.

We knew that mostly people came to have a good time. We considered ourselves in the 'fun business', so we needed to make sure people were having fun.

So, if someone was rude or in a grumpy mood, we tried to help turn that around. We made it into a bit of a game sometimes, we asked how we could turn people around and make their day really special for them, so they really felt cared for and loved and special. Those moments can make a big difference, not just in business but in someone's life too.

"The goal as a company is to have customer service that is not just the best, but legendary."

— *Sam Walton, Walmart Founder*

IT'S ALL IN THE DETAILS

It's all in the details. The little things that people often overlook.

I first learnt this when I was an accountant at PriceWaterhouseCoopers where attention to detail was extreme. Before any work was allowed to go to a client, it had to be checked by two professionals before the partners would sign off. This procedure meant two fully-qualified accountants had to sit down and work through the documents several times to make sure that it was grammatically correct, spelling was correct, and of course the that the figures were all correct. It had to all be calculated and checked before sign-off. Whilst at the time we thought it was tedious, we certainly learned how important it is to get it right. And then later on when I was a Partner in my own Accounting firm, I ensured that the quality of the work was paramount.

When I was Partner and Director of the RGM Financial Group which was smaller but with nine partners and 200 staff, the attention to detail was really important. We ensured that their name and address were spelled correctly, because no matter how good our financial advice was, if you got their personal details wrong, they would question if you had the figures wrong too.

You must be accurate in the small things, so you can be trusted with the big things.

WALK THROUGH YOUR OWN FRONT DOOR

In all my businesses, I make sure that I walk through the front door every day, even if I usually entered through the side entrance. I would walk through and peer through our customers' eyes. I'd park in the car park and walk through the front door and just observe. Observe the cleanliness, the welcoming, the signage, the pot plants. I wanted to see what our customer's see. Feel their experience. Steve Jobs said, "Get closer than ever to your customers. So close that you tell them what they need well before they realise it themselves."[20]

Customer service has to be viewed through the customers' eyes.

Can you imagine a doctor sitting in the waiting room with outdated magazines from four years ago and no coffee? They'd hate it! But that's the 'normal experience' right? Now, imagine a doctor who actually sat in their own waiting room, they'd probably reinvent the whole waiting-room experience. They'd certainly be the stand-out medical practice and everyone would recommend them.

When I was at Taxi Kitchen, we had glass doors—it was hell—we had to work very hard to keep them clean all the time. Every person's handprints ended up all over them, and we were a busy restaurant, so you could imagine how many prints would end up there.

But this door was our first impression and it had to be perfect. I'd walk through the front door often. We always ensured we had a bottle of window cleaner behind the reception desk at the restaurant. Our staff knew having clean doors was critical. I said to them, "No customer is going to mind seeing you clean a window. It's that attention to detail that shows that we care."

Better that a customer sees you cleaning than coming eye-to-eye with a filthy window. Who would want to eat in a place if the windows or front door are dirty? They'll think *if the front door is dirty, imagine what the kitchen is like!*

Walk through your own front door. Look through the eyes of your customers.

DO WHAT YOUR COMPETITORS DON'T DO

When looking after your customer, it's all about them. It's not about your product or your store, it's about them. It's about two things:

1. Solving a problem they have, or
2. Providing them with an experience/product/solution they're looking for.

So, if you can dig deep and ask lots of questions to find out what is important for them, then they will sell themselves. Some sales people get so consumed and focused on telling their customers how good their product is or how good they are, they forget it's not about them. Yes, of course, you need some credibility, and good testimonials to show how good you are, but you don't need to tell them. It's far more important to listen and ask lots of questions and keep digging deeper into what they want.

Let them do the talking. Find out what problem they're trying to solve, even if they're not aware of it themselves. It's important to see what issues you can solve, find their pain point — they'll tell you what's important. If you can react to that, then that's going to give you a sale straight away, it also it builds trust, and establishes a relationship.

All you need to do is to look at what your competitors aren't doing. Now don't just think the big things, remember it's those small touchpoints that make an enormous difference.

For example, I just did a Sales Training Course with a company that do high-end kitchen renovations, beautiful and elegant designs. They're situated in Melbourne and most of their clients are affluent. Their clients are usually people in their forties to sixties, sometimes with children at home, but they've got money to spend and they want a beautiful and stylish kitchen.

When I first started dealing with them, they had no advertising or marketing strategies, all their business came through referrals or past clients, and to their credit, they'd been running for 20 years.

It was a family business and the parents had stepped aside so their son and his wife had taken over the business and she was trying to get them to change the way things had been done. Because the son grew up in the family business, he was ingrained in the way things had always been done. So, they brought me in to coach them.

We started with simple processes. For example, when they were sending quotes, what was the follow-up? Nothing, not even a phone call. It turned out that because they were busy enough, they were failing to follow up, and their conversion rates were pretty dreadful.

So we changed the procedure around that first. We included a great follow-up at the same time their clients were checking out the quotes. They booked in a follow-up appointment to go through the proposal back in their showroom. So they got commitment upfront. So of course, their conversion rate went through the roof because they knew what they were doing, and they took immediate action.

But we didn't stop there. The next two questions were:
1. *What aren't your competitors doing?*
2. *What else could you do to get that Delight Factor?*

We focused on what they could do differently. Small things that made a big difference. Things like the smell of hot scones or homemade soup cooking on the stove. We focused on making their showroom an inviting home-style kitchen, not just a clinical kitchen. They also added small touches like good crockery and cutlery in the drawers so when clients open the drawers, it was like a home.

It's about emotional engagement, making it relatable and attractive. And let's be honest, how many kitchen showrooms have you gone into and been offered a hot scone or warm soup?

Those simple things show your attention to detail and your care factor and how you understand what kitchens are being used for. It's where families gather, especially now with open-plan house designs, usually kitchens flow into dining areas and entertaining areas.

But we didn't stop there. I asked them, "So what else aren't your competitors doing? What happens after your clients have visited your showroom?"

Through our conversation, they decided to send their clients something, just to say thanks for coming in. We went through a whole list of things. They began with the usual ideas — sending flowers, a basket of goodies or movie tickets. I said no, that's too impersonal.

I was keen to send them a voucher for a local restaurant, saying to the client: *When we renovate your kitchen, we'll be some time and because you can't use your kitchen while we're rebuilding it, here's a voucher to this wonderful restaurant so you won't need to stress about cooking.*

> Customer service shouldn't stop after you've made a sale —
> it's a continual practise with or without a sale. But having
> exceptional customer service certainly makes you sales prone.

So, we decided that it was important to dig deeper. They needed to ask an assortment of questions: favourite colours, favourite foods for shelving and cooking space, how they like to entertain etc.

Ask them about their children and how it relates to their kitchen design. Ask them specific questions, for example: *Who will be cooking in the kitchen? Do you like drinking coffee? Do you host big parties? Do you plan regular dinner parties?* Get them to talk.

These questions, if you really listen, leave some very big clues. For example, if they've told you that they love cooking Indian food, the next day get an authentic Indian selection of curries and send it via a courier to them. Imagine it's wrapped in their favourite colour and has a little note that says: *We know you love Indian food, we hope you enjoy cooking in your new kitchen.*

It's that personal touch, it's only small but, it's what your competitors aren't doing.

And also, what about a really nice postcard to them, a few days later, saying thank you for choosing us. Make it a handwritten note. It doesn't matter who writes the note, (perhaps whoever has the best handwriting in the business).

Those touchpoints makes a huge difference because your competitors will not be doing it. But I'm not suggesting you focus on your competitors for too long (just notice what they're not doing so you can provide a better experience for your customers). This is perfectly summed up by Amazon owner Jeff Bezos, "If you're competitor-focused, you have to wait until there is a competitor doing something. Being customer-focused allows you to be more pioneering."[21]

So, back to the kitchen company. After sending a little surprise to their customers, they didn't stop there. Once a kitchen was installed, they collaborated with a manufacturer that crafts beautiful wooden chopping boards. On one side the clients name was engraved, and on the other side, in a subtle way, was the kitchen company's logo. It was very discreet and elegant.

So, when their friends came over to see their beautiful new kitchen they would say "Wow, who did your kitchen?" and the owners had the company name right there.

This works for all businesses. Referrals.

When we had an accounting practice, in the very early days before people were brewing coffee, we had great cappuccinos and we trained the staff to be both an accountant and a barista. Cool, right?

When a client arrived they were blown away, they didn't expect a bunch of accountants to make mean cappuccinos and lattes. You see, we made sure we had a Barista that came in as part of a deal with a coffee company, we trained the staff every month, and they loved it. They loved the extra skillset. So not only were we giving great service to our clients, but the team loved it. It was great for upskilling, we were doing something different and our clients recognised that other accountants weren't as personable. We even wrote down how they liked their coffee so the next time they came in, we would ask, "Would you like a flat white with one sugar?"

It wasn't hard but guess what they'd talk about to their friends? They would say, "You won't believe what my accountant does, not only do we have a great tax return but they all brew really good coffee."

> *"Loyal customers, they don't just come back, they don't simply recommend you, they insist that their friends do business with you."*
>
> — *Chip Bell*

TOUCHPOINT SERVICE

So, in any business, it's these small touchpoints that matter.

What else can you do that your competitors aren't? It doesn't have to be expensive. It doesn't have to be big.

And once you're systemised, you can have that process ready to go. You start from the moment you meet them and throughout the signing up process, and all the way through. Even after business is complete.

Yes, because your business is about making a living, a successful living, not a sale.

> *"If you make a sale, you can make a living. If you make an investment of time and good service in a customer, you can make a fortune."*
>
> — *Jim Rohn*

DON'T FALL INTO THE GIVEAWAY TRAP

Now, a lot of people that I work with think they're using giveaways with their customers. They tell me that they're giving away a pen, a drink bottle, a hat or a diary. I'm not talking about your merchandise. That's something that serves you and your business brand. I'm talking about personal, intimate gifts that serve them. That they like. That's especially hand-chosen for them.

People don't really want your marketing crap. But everyone seems to promote themselves and think that's a gift, but it's not. It's a psychological shift that a lot of business owners need to make. No one likes bags stuffed with promotional material. And if they do, it's not memorable, they probably just like free stuff. But it lays around the house doing nothing.

Some businesses don't want to spend money on customers, they don't want to put money into gifts that don't have their branding attached. That's poor. For example, what's the investment in installing a kitchen, what is it? Anywhere from $20,00–$50,000 plus. What's the cost you're asking your client for? But some people are too tight to spend $100 on a client. It doesn't add up.

For those just starting out business and may not have much cashflow, it's important to begin this process anyway. Find ways you can give or little things you can do that give you the edge. Putting this in as a process gets you psychologically aligned with thinking about your client, listening to them and serving their needs.

Or add the cost in to your sale price if you're concerned about your bottom line. Just keep doing that right along the business journey so each time you're standing out from your competitors. So, you're not making price an issue.

If you have to present a business proposal — make it beautiful, include great photos, tell a story and include testimonials. Have a meeting with them and don't assume it's all about price. Build your relationship with them. Often, buying is an emotive decision.

It's been proven that when people are making decisions, 20% is logic, 80% is emotion. So focus on the individual and understand that the emotional side of business is very important. (We will deal with this subject on Emotional Intelligence in Part Three.

These little touchpoints are not only for you to get wow factors but it helps your customers' emotions. It helps them feel good about you and they want to deal with people they trust.

Having a trusted relationship enables you to explain to them why you're more expensive than your competitors and what the differences are between you and them. And if you do want to offer some sort of compromise or negotiate the price, you can. Personally, I don't like dropping the price, I don't believe in discounting, because discounts only benefit price-driven customers and I believe business isn't just a game of 'who has the lowest price'. Perhaps look at an add-on or something else you could do to win more business.

> *"Every contact we have with a customer influences whether or not they'll come back. We have to be great every time or we'll lose them."*
>
> — *Kevin Stirtz, author*

ASK FOR AND ACT ON FEEDBACK

"I think it's very important to have a feedback loop, where you're constantly thinking about what you've done and how you could be doing it better."

— *Elon Musk*

It's really important to ask and act on feedback so that you give your clients a chance to comment on what sort of service they had. You want to know if they're happy. It's better to ask them than have them complaining and telling other people, because if they're not happy, you want to be able to fix it.

Some companies don't want to know the problems, they use the head-in-the-sand approach and this is a short road to liquidation. It's great to know if there's a problem because you get a chance to fix it and that's really important.

Solving problems can also be a way to build rapport. Of course you don't need a problem in order to build rapport, but if a problem occurs you can use this as an opportunity to show that you care about how they think and feel.

Ask them for ways to improve your product or service because that feedback can help you develop what you're doing and also help understand their pain points. What is important to them might be different to what you think. Or what you think you're delivering may be different. So, you need to always ask them for feedback, because once again, that's relationship building, and it helps your business develop.

But remember the golden rule after acquiring feedback is to act on it, because there's no point asking for feedback and do nothing about it. Make sure that feedback is distributed, that your team are aware of what's working and what's not working, so you can improve.

Some staff don't want to hear feedback because it may make them feel exposed, or criticised, or doubt themselves. They might try to avoid getting feedback from clients because it might expose them and their weaknesses. This is why culture is critical. You must educate everyone that feedback makes the business better. It's all about the growth of the business and how we can improve together.

So, as long as the culture is there, it's not about blame, it's all about how we grow as a team and feedback is a positive way to know how to improve. It's about how can we use the feedback to improve what we do without laying blame.

Now I know a lot of people aren't big fans of surveys, they're busy enough already. Who wants to do more paperwork? I love to offer something like a product or an add-on. A guaranteed incentive works much better. It could be some money towards their next purchase or some goodies. But be careful of the way it's phrased, I suggest:

We really care about what you think and we value your opinion. Because we love working with you, (or because we're pleased that you bought from us), we want to know how we can do better.

Be a bit raw, it's okay to show that you care. A lot of the standard ones are bland or really clinical. Whereas, be honest, tell them that you really care and really want to know. Be genuine, I think people are more likely to respond to that.

The critical factor is, ask for feedback and act on it. Make sure your team know it too. If there's a weakness, provide training to fix it as quickly as possible. But also, get back to them, they send you out a complaint, get back fast, really fast, like that day if you can.

When I was at the Taxi Kitchen, if we had a complaint in the restaurant, we didn't get many luckily, but, when we did, someone had to get back to that person straight away. We never offered free drinks or anything else, we just listened and found out what the issue was. We'd be honest and say, "We would love for you to come back and we'll address the problem, and make sure it doesn't happen again. Give us another chance, and let me personally know when you're coming, so we can make sure you're looked after."

It's about the care, taking time to listen. Zig Ziglar said, "Statistics suggest that when customers complain, business owners and managers ought to get excited about it. The complaining customer represents a huge opportunity for more business."

Though, I'm not expecting you to get excited and high-five your staff when a customer complains, I am suggesting that you value feedback — good and bad. Act on it, make things better. Learn to use it rather than have it use you.

MAKE IT EASY

Make giving feedback easy for customers. Make it simple. Use rewards if you can, because we all want something for nothing, so if there's a reward for giving feedback, fantastic! That's a big incentive.

As I mentioned, when we first purchased Campaspe Country House it was a rundown conference centre in the country, that was really tired looking. It was shabby. So, we got in there and changed the whole culture and look. It was important to know how our customers perceived things. We asked all our guests for feedback and all the conference facilitators. We asked them if they would fill out a form on their last session, and we'd collect them before they left. We got a 100% fill out rate, it wasn't rocket-science but we knew what people loved and wanted.

We simply told them that we loved having them stay here and would love their feedback, so we can learn and improve. We asked them before they left the premises rather than sending them a feedback survey after their visit.

One lady, Caroline Shahbaz, director of Shahbaz and Stonehouse left a testimonial that sums up business to me. I'm not showing you this to brag, I'm showing you this so you can see what she says is what any business can do. But that's the thing, most don't and there is the primary problem.

Here's a testimonial that sums things up:

> "As a management consultant, it is my business and particular skill set to notice the quality of the culture of organisations. Milton continually asks for, listens to and acts on feedback and continually strives for business excellence. Milton and his team seem indefatigable in their attempt to delight their customers and to provide true service. They actually do the things the text books

say to do — figure out what the customer wants and deliver. So wonderful to see a healthy organisation not only doing it right consistently but they have almost branded a unique and personalized approach to this service industry."

Caroline Shahbaz

As she said "they actually do the things the text books say to do — *figure out what the customer wants and deliver!"*

But here's something the text books don't say: **S.EX**

S.EX = THE SURPRISE EXPERIENCE

HOW BUSINESSES GROW BIG IN SMALL WAYS

Now that you're paying attention. I'd like to talk about being a little bit cheeky, a little bit memorable. Everyone wants to be memorable, don't they? Why not be deliberate in your approach and ensure you are! How to have the ultimate S.EX — *The Surprise EXperience.*

Download the Business Background Questionnaire (BBQ) at **deanpublishing.com/smallsurprises**

One of my clients is a real estate business owner, she had a good real estate firm and wanted a business coach to help her grow her business. I didn't tell her that I have a three-strike criteria. I only work with people based on three important factors.

Is the person coachable?
Can I make a difference to your business?
Am I going to enjoy working with you?

So to know this, I asked her lots of really big questions, her goals and ambitions and what she wanted to achieve and why. It became quite a personal conversation, as most business coaching interviews can, and I really listened to her needs and wants.

Now this client had a business plan. She wanted to get the business systemised so she could spend six months in Italy within two years' time. That was her immediate goal. She loved food and wanted to live in Italy and embed herself in the culture and flavours of their cuisine.

We decided to work together because she was ready and I knew I could help her create positive change. When clients sign up, I like to send them a gift. So armed with my notes from our conversation, I went shopping. I got a really lovely basket in her favourite colour and added in an authentic Italian cookbook, quite an obscure one which I'm sure she didn't have. I put in some Italian-made chocolate, some olives and some wine. Everything she loved.

When she received the basket, she rang me up immediately.

"I have never received a gift that's just so..*me!*" she said, "everything in the basket is so ME!"

She said, "I've been given gift baskets before and most of the stuff I never use or I give away. If you understand me that well from one meeting and you went to all that trouble, imagine what you can for my business."

This small surprise gave me instant credibility in her eyes. And it wasn't complicated or expensive. That whole basket cost me $80 for thousands of dollars a year.

Of course, I made sure that it was delivered the next day, not weeks later. If I could, I would have gotten it there within an hour. Simple things, matter a whole lot. They are worth the effort, sure it takes a bit of time but isn't your client worth that?

A lot of companies use automated emails, and even fewer send cards, parcels or packages. Automated emails aren't personal or surprising — they're overdone and most we don't even open. In fact, a 2021 report showed the average click through rate for email marketing is as low as 2.6%.[22]

What are the chances of someone opening a beautiful gift? Pretty good, don't you think?

Sure, one is a targeted client and the other may be a prospect, but the point is — being memorable or surprising a client isn't really done via an automated email campaign, it's about being personal. Business can be an intimate exchange if you think about other people.

> *"The key is to set realistic customer expectations, and then not to just meet them, but to exceed them — preferably in unexpected and helpful ways."*
>
> — ***Richard Branson***

FIND OUT WHAT'S UNIQUE ABOUT YOU AND EXPLOIT IT

How can business owners really know their point of difference? If you do, you can create your first impressions around your unique point of difference. Knowing your brand. Knowing how you stand out is vital.

My clients have a full 13-page document to work through, this helps me know their exact niche and target their market from the beginning. Why not try to hit the bullseye first, right?

I often hear, "What is my/our niche?" and "How can I/we identify our unique selling point?"

There's are always different ways to do business. Thinking outside-the-square or brainstorming how you can be different is a great place to start.

Spend five minutes asking yourself:
- *How is my business different?*
- *What do we do that our competitors don't do?*
- *How can we be memorable?*
- *What matters most to our customers?*
- *What are our Delight Factors?*

When I was CEO at Taxi Kitchen, we did something that people classed as a little outrageous. We changed the wine list from international to ONLY local Victorian. People, including staff and stakeholders said, "We can't do that. People are going to hate that. They'll want the wine from all over the world."

But I thought: *We're at Fed Square. We're in Victoria. We'll educate the team so that when someone asks for a wine from South Australia or France, we'll say, "We have a similar wine from Victoria that is just as great. Would you like to try that instead?"*

We educated our staff in wine knowledge. We even took them on trips to our local wineries. We knew that not every client would be happy at the beginning but we would educate them about our local regions.

If you want a Margaret River wine, then go to Margaret River. But this is a great town and we support our local winemakers. Often, we could tell our clients that they were sitting in the same restaurant as the winemaker. Because often, the winemakers were dining in the restaurant. They loved that we were supporting their wine and were knowledgeable about their product. Our best customers were the other Victorian winemakers, producers and Victorian tourism came back on board and started having functions at our restaurant because we were promoting Victorian products. Same with the dishes.

We became known through tourism and wine festivals. And our staff were able to explain all about our different wines and regions and really showcase Victoria. This became an easy selling point.

At first, it seemed outrageous to people. Why wouldn't we offer wines from all over the world? Because we weren't from all over the world — we were in the centre, and the heart of Melbourne. Our mantra was — let's not do what all the other restaurants are doing. Let's be proud of our city, our local producers and support Victorian tourism. It's all about being local but thinking globally.

This business model gave us an edge with government, Tourism bodies, the Melbourne Food and Wine Festival and the Victorian wine industries.

PUT PEOPLE IN THEIR GENIUS ZONE TO ENHANCE ECX

It's important to put the right people with the right skillsets in the right places. It enhances customer service in a natural and beneficial way.

I remember once, we had the most amazing waitress, let's call her Tracey. Tracey was an amazing ray of sunshine, she just beamed and radiated joy wherever she went. She was fabulous at explaining the menu, she was so animated and knowledgeable that she mesmerised people. The guests would just look in awe at her, they just loved her and they would have done anything for her; she could have sold them anything.

You rarely see that, someone so engaged, she was wonderful with everyone on the team and so we promoted her to restaurant manager. This decision proved to be a huge failure because she was a people person, but she couldn't manage people. She hated delegating, she couldn't direct, she couldn't pull people up when they were doing the wrong thing, and she was the worst restaurant manager. She didn't like it and neither did anyone else.

She hated the team meetings, she hated doing reports, it was a huge disaster. Here was this fabulous, engaged waiter who was just the best at her job, so much that she got promoted. But she wasn't in her genius zone. She didn't like managing, she liked waiting tables and looking after customers.

This was such a big lesson for me. It made me realise that not everybody wants to be promoted, some people want to remain doing what they love. In their own genius zone.

It's important to give people opportunities and allow them to make mistakes, to let them to grow and develop. But don't presume they want what you think they want, ask them what they like. Ask specific questions like: *Do you have other special interests that could help the business? What else would you like to learn? What sort of training would you like?*

We will go deeper into this in the Part 2 (Team and Team Motivation) but the key point is:

The best customer experiences happen when staff or team members are able to provide that in a way that they LOVE.

Putting team members in their genius zone enhances customer service.

THE ANSWER IS ALWAYS 'YES'

When a client asks for something, how many times can you say 'yes' to their request?

Our staff were trained in the power of yes. Not as a gimmick but as a genuine service. Many times, people aren't asking for big things, they are asking for little things: water for the table, a spare toothbrush, an extra seat at the table, directions on where to park, a pen.

Systems are great, but they aren't supposed to be rigid guidelines that neglect the client. They are supposed to support the power of yes.

Let me tell you what a packet of Kool Mints once did for my business.

When I was running Campaspe Country House we had a regular business client and old friend called Derek. He was the type that loved to combine business and fun at the same time. A business man and a great networker. He often brought business guests and friends with him and loved good food and wine. We always made sure that he was well looked after and that his guests were happy. We knew that he loved the way we looked after his guests.

One night, Derek and his guests were having a few social drinks and playing pool together. We were serving them regularly and asking them if there was anything else we could do for them. The night became quite late.

When I came in to check if everything was going well for Derek, I asked him, "Is there anything else we can do for you, Derek?"

He said "No thank you, you and your team have done a great job all night."

However, whilst I was in the room, I overheard them talking. They were sharing their fond memories of the lollies called Kool Mints. They each had a different story and commented that they had not seen or tasted them for years. So I discreetly set to work.

Now, it was at night and we were in the country. No shops were open and we didn't stock Kool Mints. I rang a friend of mine, George, who owned the corner store. We were a big client of his and George understood good customer service.

"Hi George. It's Milton from Campaspe Country House. Look, I know it's late and I'm really sorry to call you but I need to ask a favour."

I explained to him that we had an important client staying with us and asked if he stocked Kool Mints. I explained that I really wanted to over-deliver. As I said, George understood exceptional customer service. He said, "Meet me at the shop in 10 minutes."

He jumped in his car and drove back to the shop. I met him there and together we laughed about the crazy things good business owners are willing to do to wow their clients. I thanked him profusely and arrived back at Campaspe Country House with not one but two packets of Kool Mints.

I presented Derek and his guests with the treasured Kool Mints and his jaw fell to the floor.

"What?!" he gasped. His shocked face spoke more than his words.

Now, the interesting thing about this story (besides the fact, it's true) is that Derek never ever forgot about those Kool Mints. He told everybody about it. In fact, getting him some late night Kool Mints resulted in more referrals from Derek than I can remember.

Now of course we served him in numerous ways, we had ensured that his food was exquisite and his choice of beverages were first class, but in many ways he expected this. He paid for this and didn't expect anything less than top-shelf service. But he didn't expect the Kool Mints, and that's why they remained in his memory — because they were a surprise, they exceeded his expectations and made him smile!

⚜ FOUNDATIONS TO DELIGHT, ⚜ DISRUPT AND DELIVER

1. Make a good first impression — smiles, systems, scripts, service and surprises.
2. Create a culture
3. Have a vision
4. Look after your environment and attitude
5. Use extreme customer service
6. Do what your customers don't do
7. Ask and act on feedback
8. Use S.EX — the Surprise Experience

THE TOP 3 PAIN POINTS I GUARANTEE YOU'LL HEAR

No matter how great you are as a person and business owner, no matter how incredible your business product or service is — if you're in business, you're going to encounter problems of some sort. We often refer to these problems or obstacles as "pain points". Sticky places where people resist or have blockages of resistance.

What turns a good business owner into a great business owner, is the ability to identify and solve other people's pain points. If you develop a talent for listening and solving pain points, you're already ahead of the game. In fact, you're setting yourself up to win.

In my experience as a business leader, there are three major hurdles that you'll always come up against — three pain points. They are:

TIME	MONEY	TEAM

These 3 pain points always seem to arise within the common issues I hear from my clients. Things like:

- I don't have enough time
- I don't have a reliable team
- I don't have enough money
- Our culture needs fixing
- We need better resources
- If my staff were doing this or that, then we wouldn't be in this situation.

They also say things would different if they had these things.

- If I had more time I would fix the sign out of the front of my business
- If I had a team I could rely on, then I'd go on a holiday
- If we made more money, I'd hire a business coach
- If we weren't so small, it would be easier for us to make a difference

These all seem legitimate complaints and very often they are true. However if you want to grow your business you have to understand that these pain points are common. These pain points are often universal and your clients will have them too. They will even use them against you. If you don't have a good awareness of pain points and if you haven't got good strategies in place to combat them when they arise (both within you and them) — then you are destined to run your business by default and not actively mould it to your benefit.

Let's go through each pain point and identify them.

PAIN POINT #1: TIME

We live in a frantic world and nowadays the pace of life is extreme. We're all time-poor to some degree. We are all juggling a long to-do list. It often feels like there's not enough hours in the day, and things move so quickly. Because of this extreme pace, which no one can truly keep pace with — it becomes a matter of priorities and planning.

The Australian Bureau of Statistics released a General Social Survey that revealed 45% of women and 36% of men were 'always' or 'often' rushed or pressed for time.[23] And I suspect those statistics are growing every year. Yep, 'the lucky country' is feeling the unlucky time pinch. Work-life balance is tilting in a lopsided way more than ever.

You've probably heard a lot of speakers talk about this subject of time. Many say things like, "You have the same amount of time as Einstein, Anthony Robbins and Beyonce — but the question is what are you doing with it?" Have you heard that before? Personally, I've never found these style of "motivational" talks helpful. If anything, you just feel like an under-achiever that can't manage your time well.

And though, yes, we all do have the same amount of time, we don't all share equal amounts of opportunity, support, environmental factors and money. For example, someone who needs to walk a mile to obtain internet access has a different time issue than someone who has Wi-Fi in their home. Or someone that has a learning disability may take longer to read a business report than another person who is a speed reader. Someone delivering advertising flyers on a motorbike is going to be more productive than the person who can't afford a bike and has to walk.

Time is only equal in terms of its actuality on the clock but it's not equal in other ways.

Knowing how to use *your time* to achieve *your own results* is the key. Not to compare it to other people.

Einstein may have been a remarkable mind, but he was an absent father. He was rich but left all his royalties and academic papers to the university whilst his family succumbed to poverty. In other words, he used his time for achievement, not family. That was his choice.

But many of us don't want to live a lopsided life and put work above all else. We want to use our time in a balanced but productive way. In an optimal way. A way that works for us.

So, how I combat the 'time-poor' issue and help my clients and customers through is by firstly using a very practical measure: we use a diary. We sit down, and plan what is going to happen during the week ahead. We allocate time during the week for the main things required in order for them to do their job. But before we do that, we do the most important thing which is — work out what they like doing, what's productive, what they don't like doing and what's not productive. Sounds simple I know, but who is actually doing it?

Because here's the thing: there will be things on your list to-do that you don't really have to do. But often we are so time-poor that we even put planning our time effectively on the backburner.

Let's begin this together.

DIARY BREAKDOWN

✓ **What's important?** Focus on these as a priority.

✕ **What's not important?** List them but attend to them after you've finished the important jobs

✓ **What's productive?** Focus on doing what works.

✕ **What's not productive?** Only do them if it's absolutely necessary.

✓ **What do I like to do?** Find a way to do this more if it's also productive.

✕ **What do I dislike doing?** Delegate to someone else or ditch.

Sometimes people get obsessed with doing the easy stuff or doing stuff that isn't productive. If it's not important or productive, why even do it? Either delegate or just find ways to ditch it. In many cases, we can delegate tasks to somebody who can do it better. It could be someone in the team, or outsourced to someone with more expertise.

So with a *default diary*, one should assess what's important and what's not important, and what you should be doing, and what you should be delegating. In order to Delight, Disrupt and Deliver you have to know where to focus and why. You must come to the realisation that you need to: DECIDE — DO — DELEGATE or DITCH.

To receive your free Diary Template go to **deanpublishing.com/smallsurprises**

4 TIME MANAGEMENT FACTORS TO MAKE YOU X10 MORE EFFICIENT

DECIDE
What's important or not.
What's productive?

DO
What do I do?

DELEGATE
What do I delegate and
to who?

DITCH
What can I ditch?

DECIDE — What's important or not. What's productive?

....

....

....

....

....

....

....

....

....

....

....

DO — What do I do?

....

....

....

....

....

....

....

....

....

DELEGATE — What do I delegate and to who?

....

....

....

....

....

....

....

....

....

DITCH — What can I ditch?

....

....

....

....

....

....

....

....

....

SETTING YOUR WEEK UP FOR SUCCESS

It's important to set your days and weeks up for success. Otherwise, without planning for success, it won't come knocking at your door, right?

I suggest to my clients to use a default diary or a planner every night, to schedule their next day. What I've done in my offices with all my team members, is to set up a rule that everyone sits down in the last ten minutes of the day and writes what they're doing tomorrow. Listing it in point form is enough. I asked them to leave it on their desk, and if I walked around at the end of the day, and they didn't have that list, then I made them accountable. I asked them, why?

And that makes a big difference, because subconsciously, overnight you're thinking about it. You've actually gone through the process of planning your day in advance for tomorrow, and subconsciously or consciously, you're ready to take action and hit the ground running.

This small habit soon begins to saves time and increase productivity. You already know what's important and what's not before you begin your working day.

I encourage people to set up a default diary and begin to plan what has to be done for the rest of the week or even the following week or month. Although future planning isn't on the overnight accountability list, it's important to think beyond the general day-to-day activities. Planning ahead in your diary is like setting yourself up to win.

The same goes with telephone calls. Take them when it suits you. You don't have to be available 24-7 for everyone's telephone calls. As long as you get back to people and there's a message. If it's on your mobile phone, you can even send an automatic message back to them. If you have a receptionist or a PA or someone who can take the call for you, that's even better of course. If you've got a PA who can manage your time, that's brilliant. But if you don't have that, you can still do it through your own phone system, or through your receptionist too.

MAKE TIME MANAGEMENT A HABIT

Making time management a habit makes you more prone to success.

To be honest, I'm not naturally a person who likes to make a list. Often, I have to force myself do it and remind myself why I do it. But because I like to be in charge of my life and I want to get results, I think of the end result and that works for me. I love outcomes.

There's nothing overly clever about time management. There's no extra hours in a day, it's about *maximising* those hours. I find that doing 'time blocks' is more efficient than trying to do everything at once and getting distracted and overwhelmed.

REFLECTION

The key to planning is really about being aware of things and the diary makes this visible. A default diary shows you where you plan on going and how you plan on getting there. Simple but powerful if you like results.

If you don't take time to reflect on what you're doing and why — then you'll stay on the hamster wheel of life without truly assessing why you've spent years running around and around in circles wasting your own precious time. Yes, until you actually SEE what the heck you've been doing, you'll keep running in circles. Maybe it's time to give up the hamster wheel and get on the express to success, which means managing your time without dancing to the beat of other people's drums. Be deliberate. Be strategic. Be accountable.

But it's not just because it's helped me that I advise people to use a diary. Research supports the notion that keeping a diary has many positive impacts, and not only on how we manage time.

At the University of Texas in Austin, psychologist and researcher James Pennebaker contends that regular journaling strengthens immune cells and he also suggests that writing about stressful events helps you come to terms with them because it reduces stress and aids our physical and mental wellbeing.[24] So, you don't have to use your diary to simply manage time, you can vent your stress and write about things that are important to you.

Now, I know what you're thinking: "Milton, writing things down isn't my thing, sure it may reduce my stress, but so will a massage and a wine!"

Good point, I love a good red too, but there's something wine can't do that a diary can.

YOU LEARN FROM REFLECTION

According to a study conducted by Harvard Business School, participants who journaled at the end of the day had a 25% increase in performance when compared with a control group who did not journal. The researchers conclude that "Our results reveal reflection to be a powerful mechanism behind learning, confirming the words of American philosopher, psychologist, and educational reformer John Dewey: 'We do not learn from experience...we learn from reflecting on experience.'"[25]

Dutch scientist Marije Elferink-Gemser[26] arrived at the same conclusion. After studying the attributes that help people get through performance plateaus the scientists found that "Reflection is...a key factor in expert learning and refers to the extent to which individuals are able to appraise what they have learned and to integrate these experiences into future actions, thereby maximizing performance improvements."

- **Clarify your thoughts and feelings**
  Take a few minutes to write down your thoughts or your to-do list for tomorrow to help you gain mental clarity about situations and what to do. Even bullet-point writing is enough to gain clarity.

- **Solve problems more effectively**
  Usually, we problem solve from a left-brained dominance. But sometimes the answer can only be found by engaging right-brained creativity. Writing unlocks these other capabilities and give us the opportunity for surprise solutions to appear. (Okay, maybe wine does this too!)

- **Resolve conflicts**
Writing about misunderstandings or problems can help you to understand another's point of view and come up with a sound resolution.

- **Plan and track patterns**
Writing things down allows you to see and track patterns, trends and even personal improvement and growth over time. It can help you see how far you've actually come through the year.

- **Improves your cognitive functioning**
According to research published in the *Journal of Experimental Psychology: General,* expressive writing reduces intrusive thoughts and improves working memory.[27]

- **Reduces rumination and promotes action**
You stop going over things in your mind and begin taking laser-focused action in the right direction. Researchers published in the *Journal of Experimental Psychology* found that journaling before bed decreases over-thinking, rumination, and worry and allows you to fall asleep faster.[28]

- **Feeds your unconscious mind positively**
Chess champion and grandmaster of martial arts, Josh Waitzkin discusses his journaling strategy for performance and success. He says, "My journaling system is based around studying complexity. Reducing the complexity down to what is the most important question. Sleeping on it, and then waking up in the morning first thing and pre-input brainstorming on it. So I'm feeding my unconscious material to work on, releasing it completely, and then opening my mind and riffing on it."[29]

And his isn't the only one that taps into the power of his unconscious mind. The founder of LinkedIn, Reid Hoffman jots things down things for his mind to work on overnight. People like Oprah, Benjamin Franklin, Thomas Edison, Andy

Warhol, Brendan Burchard, Time Ferriss, Lady Gaga and others all use diaries, and do you think they aren't busy too?

Having a diary is like having a torch in the dark — it draws your eye towards what to focus on and this helps you step forward on the path ahead.

> *"Keeping a personal journal, a daily in-depth analysis and evaluation of your experiences is a high-leverage activity that increases self-awareness and enhances all the endowments and the synergy among them."*
>
> — *Stephen R. Covey*

TIME IS YOUR INTERNAL ACCOUNT

Imagine you had a bank account that deposited $86,400 each morning. Now imagine that that same bank account doesn't allow you to hold the money overnight for you to use the next day. So in fact, every night as your head hits the pillow, it cancels the amount you failed to use during the day. It can be a disturbing or exciting thought depending on how you look at it.

So the obvious question would be, what would you do with that money? You'd draw out every dollar out and use it every day, right?

We all have such a bank. Its name is Time. Every morning, it credits you with 86,400 seconds. Every night it writes it off. But you get to spend it however you wish.

Now, imagine that you add your team's working time? How much time is amplified into a focused business direction? For example, if your team spend eight hours at work a day, then that is a time bank account and you get to spend it. So where do you focus that time? On things that get you ahead of the game, right? On activities that move your business forward and upwards. It's up to you.

PAIN POINT #2: MONEY. MONEY, MONEY.

"I love money. I love everything about it. I bought some pretty good stuff. Got me a $300 pair of socks. Got a fur sink. An electric dog polisher. A gasoline powered turtleneck sweater. And, of course, I bought some dumb stuff, too."

— *Steve Martin*

A lot of people's money mindset is very much like Steve Martin's joke, yet it's real. The pain point of money is a big one. It's often highly charged with emotion too. You have a relationship with money whether you like it or not. Some people have very good relationships with money and others find it overwhelming and prefer to ignore money issues.

I'm amazed at the number of people in business that don't really understand their finances. I have met many people that are actually running good businesses, and have been doing it in some cases for many years, but when it comes to drilling down into their profit and loss statement — they run a mile. Many think that the money-side of their business is for their bookkeeper or accountant. They don't realise that they hold the money strings and how critical it is to be able to test and measure what your business is doing.

Do not put your head in the sand, you won't find money there.

YOU CAN'T MEASURE WHAT YOU DON'T LOOK AT

We have to take off the 'I-don't-want-to-discuss-finances' goggles and have a good look at the profit and loss and cashflow of your business.

When working with my clients, I make sure they are obtaining regular financial reports, and we look at them together every month. That way, we can begin to assess what they do each month, and what they did the same time last month, and last year. We also work on a budget for them. Now, most small businesses don't do that one simple activity. Yes, it sounds boring but I like to remind people about how exciting it is to actually make money.

I'm amazed at the number of sizable small businesses that give up their financial power. They remain in financial denial. I hear things like, "Our accountant does that", or "I'll ask my bookkeeper". Now, of course make sure your accountant or bookkeeper are doing their job, but if you're not communicating with them or understanding how to financially proof your business, then you're not flexing your financial capacity.

There are those who try to do everything themselves, the finances, the sales, the cleaning, the ordering. In many instances, I sit down with the owners and see what it costs them to hire a bookkeeper. Often business owners are better off hiring someone to do their accounts whilst they use that time to sell or do what they're good at. The question is: how much more could you make per hour selling or doing more of what you're good at, or bringing in more customers compared to paying a bookkeeper? Where is your time balancing?

What you need to do now is learn how to use those reports. Yes, have a bookkeeper or an accountant, but do not give your financial responsibility over to them. Become the maker of your money and find ways to increase the profit and your ability to make good financial decisions.

"Opportunity is missed by most people because it is dressed in overalls and looks like work."

— *Thomas Edison*

MONEY MADE SIMPLE

To assess your reports, there's really only two or three things you really need to worry about.

MONEY IN — MARGIN — MONEY OUT

MONEY IN	MARGIN IN BETWEEN	MONEY OUT
INCOME, SALES	PROFIT	DIRECT EXPENSES
(PEOPLE PAYING YOU)	(WHERE YOU MAKE MONEY)	(YOU PAYING)

Money In (Income): What are your sales? What is your gross income?

Money Out (Direct Expenses): What are your direct costs? If you're in retail, it may be the product that you're selling, what does that cost you? What did you buy it for and minus that from the sales price.

If you're in a service industry and sell hours, then it's the sales you and your team make less what you pay them in wages. This is your gross profit. In some cases, businesses have both. For example, a motor vehicle repair shop. They have parts and they have labour, so look at the sales less direct labour (so not the admin people, it's just people who are working on jobs) plus materials, equals your gross profit.

Margin: Now if you concentrate on the margin in between your income and expenses, that is the most important part of running a business!

Focus on the margin in between 'Money In' and 'Money Out' with your financials. It will make a huge difference.

Once you've got this, you can estimate, things like your telephone bill, office expenses, rent. That's not going to change too much, so you can budget these. And sure, at some stage you want to make sure that you've negotiated the best rent, the right telephone system, the right computer and software system, but once you've done that, that's not going to change every month, you need to remain focused on the margin in between Money In and Money Out. That's where the business can grow and develop the best. It helps you remain focused on what works — which is PROFIT!

> I have developed a very simple profit/loss template that you can download for FREE at **deanpublishing.com/ smallsurprises**

EXAMPLE OF A PROFIT/LOSS STATEMENT

Business Name

1st July 2020 to 30th June 2021

Revenue	
Gross Sales	

Cost of Goods Sold	
Beginning Inventory	
Add: Purchases	
Direct Labor	
Direct Expenses	
Less: Ending Inventory	
Cost of Goods Sold	
Gross Profit (Loss)	

Expenses	
Advertising	
Bad Debts	
Bank Charges	
Depreciation	
Employee Benefit Programs	
Insurance	
Interest	
Postage	
Rent	
Repairs and Maintenance	
Telephone	
Vehicle Expenses	
Wages	
Total Expenses	
Net Operating Income	

Other Income	
Interest Income	
Total Other Income	
Net Income (Loss)	

CHARGE PROPERLY

Where a lot of people go wrong is that they don't charge for their work properly. If you have an employee but you're only charging out a six-hour day instead of an eight-hour day — who is absorbing the cost of the other two hours? Your business is. You are!

You lost two hours during the day simply because you weren't accurate. If you are under-charging and you feel like you can't charge it to your customer, then get it on the job cost sheet first. If you're going to write it off, that's a decision you can make down the track, but if you don't count it, you don't have that decision to make.

It's not complicated, you can easily break it down for someone with no financial training, once they know how to evaluate it. With my clients, we keep it very simple and focus on how we can improve the margin without compromising quality or productivity. Yes, inside that margin is where the magic lies.

Small businesses tend to have lower survival rates and more volatile revenues than larger firms, many are more vulnerable and less resilient to downturns in the economy. Yet, they play a significant role in the Australian economy. The small business sector accounts for almost half of the total employment in the private non-financial sector and over a third of production. Importantly, they contribute to local economies by bringing growth, innovation, jobs and income to their communities. It is therefore important for the health and sustainability of local communities that small businesses continue to thrive and to do this they need to understand how to **make the cash flow.**

So many small businesses could be making a big profit but if they're not making and collecting money, they can go broke. They might have slow payers or bad debts, so they need a system in place to make sure they can efficiently get money in.

Personally, when I take on a new client, we set the terms upfront. If you don't discuss money and you don't have procedures in place and follow through, it can all blow up very quickly. Money can get sucked into business black holes when you're not looking.

For example, I ask my clients to pay me a month in advance before I even start work. When I share this with other business owners, they often say, "oh, we can't do that". But all my clients do it and I've never lost one client over my payment terms. That's just the way I operate, and because I've set it that way from day one, people get it. If you set the parameters, then it's easy for everyone to play and no one has the play the guessing game.

You can also create a payment form, so every month that same payment comes out at the same time — and you get paid. In other words, set your business up to guarantee cashflow. You need a healthy, growing business, not to chase debt. It also helps establish a relationship of trust, you know when you're being paid and they know they're getting a great service. So that creates a better relationship for both the client and you.

I also request that my clients sign up for a minimum of 12 months because this creates the greatest business transformation. I'm not promising an overnight quick fix. It's coaching people to run a better business, to become a better business person. When you use those skills, you see a future, not just your current circumstance. And I explain to people that I want them to build a profitable enterprise that can work without them. In that way, they've got a choice — they can build a business to either sell or step back from, or it can run wonderfully without them. This way, they get maximum value, it frees them up to do other things, spend more time with the family, or play golf, learn another skill or build another business.

MONEY MINDSET

We often hear a lot about the money mindset. Many people have subconscious or conscious money ideas that block them their success or block them from going and achieving their full potential.

I often ask my clients to tell me the thoughts or ideas that spring to mind when they think about money. Many people report that they're often embarrassed to talk about money. Now of course, in a social setting you don't tell people how much money you're making or what money means to you; that's inappropriate. But if you're in business, you want to make money. You need to make money to keep your business going. Yet money isn't the #1 reason you're in business. If you're going to tell me that you're in business solely to make money, you've missed the point. But if you think a business can operate without profit, then you've missed the point too.

Most people go into business because they love what they do. But I always remind people that unless you're making money, you can't afford to do what you love every day. You can't afford to give the better service, you can't afford to grow your business, you can't live well. You won't have a business if you don't focus on money and make sure it's running profitably. So, you've got to have a healthy respect for money.

"The person who doesn't know where his next dollar is coming from usually doesn't know where his last dollar went."

— *Unknown*

WHY I NEVER DISCOUNT

Many people buy on price. Yes, it's all too often a discount-oriented market place. If you go out there to be the cheapest product on the market, that only works if you're a Coles or a Woolworths, because most small businesses can't get into the competitive pricing market without going bankrupt.

I often request people to not enter the discount rat-race unless they want to be known as the cheapest or have a crazy cheap product to sell that still gives them a profit.

But people don't always buy the cheapest product, and if they do, it's because they're discount shoppers, but let's be honest, discount shoppers are not going to be loyal. They're only looking for the cheapest and the moment you're not the cheapest, they'll toss you out for someone else. They're not really a client you want, because they're always going to be chasing the lowest price. They won't be coming back to you. If you're a small business, you're not big enough to be a discount mogul, so you shouldn't be positioning your brand in that field.

You need to show your customers that they're making an investment, that their good money is worth spending with you, that it's going to solve their pain or their problems. Or perhaps it's going to create a great lifestyle for them or give them a great solution.

Yes, it's got to be value for money, but you've also got to make other issues more important than the bottom line price.

Of course, if you're selling a product for example, it needs to be better than its cheaper alternative, it needs to be higher-quality and offer something much better. But this also allows you to step up your pricing and appeal to a market that aren't solely discount shoppers.

ARE YOU CHARGING WHAT YOU'RE WORTH?

I often say to my clients, "Put your prices up!"

The typical response is, "Oh no, we can't do that."

The people who worry most about price increases are going out of business.

"What happened the last time you put your prices up?" I ask.

"Um…well…nothing."

"How many clients did you lose?"

"Well, only one." (There's often a nervous laugh about here.)

This is usually where I level with them and say, "Look, you're in business. If you're not losing some people when you put your price up, you haven't got a future owner."

People usually look at me stunned.

"You should be able to sell your business as an investment. In many cases, if you increase it by 20%, and lose 5% of your clients, it's fine. You've got less work to do for a much better return."

Maybe out of thousands of customers, you'll get one or two complaints. And yes, that could happen. But there's always somebody that's going to complain no matter what. That's a given in business. But if it's a very low percentage, it's not a problem in the long run. With excellent customer service you should woo your customers. And if they leave, at least you know they're leaving you based on price. But when most people lose customers, it's because of something else, something hasn't been done or you let them down in some other way.

Often it's just a fear that stops people putting their prices up. Fear of losing business, fear of embarrassment.

One of my recent clients is a very well-respected allied health practitioner. We were discussing profit margins and I asked him to consider increasing his price by 15%. I'd actually done some research for him and rang around some competitors asking their price. By ringing around I discovered that he was the cheapest in his area. Now, this guy won the best practitioner in the state that year and had a fabulous reputation for being professional. He had been in his practice for 20 years. Fully-established but not increasing in profit at all.

I said, "James, you've got to put your prices up."

James literally gasped and said, "Oh, I can't do that!"

"What happened the last time you put your prices up?"

"Well, nothing. But I don't think I should put my prices up."

"Any complaints?" I asked.

"Well, no," he said.

"Do people come to you because you're the cheapest?" I asked.

"No, they come because I'm good." James said.

"Well, look at this. Here's the list of competitors in your area, and what they're charging. Are they better than you?" I handed him the list.

"Well no, I'm far better than any of them."

"So why are you the cheapest? Why won't you put your prices up?"

Still reluctant, he eventually increased his price. Not one single complaint. He didn't lose any customers whatsoever, but I still couldn't get him to go up the full 15%, I only got him up 8% which frustrated the hell out of me, but at least he had increased the price.

So, the next time we met I said, "Okay, it's your business. I'm only here to coach you, but I want you to review your prices after six months rather than twelve months."

"I've never done that before," he said.

"Good. I like that you've never done it before. That's fantastic. It allows you to try something different."

We agreed.

Often owners are more obsessed with price than their customers, but it's got to be value for money. If you charge too much and don't deliver, that's not good business.

Many years ago, one of my roles with an accounting firm, was to buy fees from other accountants. Buying fees basically means purchasing a parcel of client fees from an accounting firm that is ready to retire or move on to another business opportunity. It accelerates growth by instantly adding more clients and the fees that they are charged. Many times we'd buy fees from businesses that weren't operating very well. They were often single operators who had been in the business for a long time. They wanted to get out. So we'd look at buying their fees and give them good money for it. What we commonly came across was the fact that they were under-charging.

So we would go in and just increase their fees by 10% or small amounts gradually. It was a whole different service we were offering and we were much more professional, so we raised prices about 10%. We would help the owners manage their business. We would grow their business. We helped them make more money. We helped them with insurance. We helped them with investments. It was a whole range of services, so we needed to charge more for that.

In one business, we lost 10% of the clients because we doubled the fees. And from then on, the business began to run smoothly. It worked like a dream because we made more money for less work, and it was value for money.

> *"Money is only a tool. It will take you wherever you wish, but it will not replace you as the driver."*
>
> **— Ayn Rand**

———————

Unfortunately, many businesses in Australia fail to thrive. According to a report from Business and Economics at University of Melbourne, 97% of startup businesses exit or fail to grow. And out of those, a staggering 60% of small businesses stop operation within the first three years of their startup journey.[30]

But what I find more interesting than the statistics is the reason behind them. WHY so many businesses are not making it through the business stages of growth.

The Australian Centre for Business Growth investigated this exact thing. They looked at *why*. They looked specifically at small and medium-sized Australian businesses and collected data from CEOs who had been part of a company failure or whose small or medium companies had failed. Here are the top reasons why most small or medium businesses failed.

TOP REASONS FOR SMALL MEDIUM BUSINESS FAILURE

25% = Insufficient leadership and management and planning and execution.

17% = Inadequate market research, marketing, sales

14% = Poor financial management

13% = Underestimating the impact of externalities

11% = Poor governance structures re partners, family

7% = Product or service problems

6% = Poor management of people

4% = Inexperienced CEO

3% = Wrong strategy or poor implementation

TOTAL = 100%[31]

Notice the top three reasons for failure:

#1: *Leadership.*
If you're entering into business, you simply MUST advance yourself in leadership skills.

#2: *Inadequate market research and sales.*
In other words, not knowing the market properly and probably not charging enough.

#3: *Poor financial management.*
Speaks for itself — head in the sand approach.

Here are 8 additional tips for surviving and even thriving during the economic downturn:

1. Advance in your leadership skills.
If you're in business, you must always grow and learn more about leadership. It begins (and ends) with you. Leadership skills can be taught and you must have the courage to advance in them to stay on top and thrive in business.

2. Define your mission and goals
Think about why you started your business in the first place. What is it that you want to offer? Who are your customers? What do you want to achieve? Are your business goals aligned with your personal goals? Have you lost sight of these?

3. Regain your focus
You should always have a focus. Your focus may shift from time to time, but you cannot lose focus. Too many businesses try to be all things to everyone by servicing too many customers or over diversifying their offerings. Define your core business, understand your core customers and focus on what you are good at.

4. Determine who your customers are
Getting the right customers is far more important than having the most customers. Determine who your customers are and focus on servicing them. Too many businesses try to service as many customers as they can to generate revenue even if it means straying from their core business, over extending their resources and putting in more effort than would be required if the customer was a good fit to begin with.

5. Remember no man is an island

You cannot do everything yourself. You need to build and nurture a strong team to build a robust and sustainable business. Surround yourself with the best people you can find to help you implement your mission, keep the cogs turning, and deliver. Your people are your business's most important assets — treat them that way.

6. Cash flow is king

At the end of the day, it is the bottom line that counts. What the books say doesn't matter if there is no money in the bank. Find out where you are making or losing money. Identify the products and services that are costing you money rather than earning you money and don't do business with customers that take their time to pay or don't pay at all. They are not money in the bank! If financials are not your forte, hire someone to do it for you.

7. Service, service, service

Never let service slip. Great service differentiates one business from another that has the same offering. You want to create an exceptional customer experience because that is what will keep your customers returning to you instead of your competitor down the road. When the going gets tough, dig deep and find ways to improve service levels. When the going gets tough, small businesses get left behind. Customer retention is pivotal, especially in tougher economic times. Adding value is one of the best and easiest ways of ensuring that your customers do not stray.

As a business owner, you should carefully consider what your customers need and think strategically about how you can deliver this to them seamlessly and at a fair price. Focus on the little things such as optimising your levels of customer service, making it easy for people to source and pay for your products and services, getting to know your customers better and personalising their experience when it comes to interacting with you and your business. The customer experience is what keeps them engaged and coming back, even when money is tight.

When your customers receive exceptional service, and feel that they are getting excellent value, they become loyal and will also start recommending your business to others. You cannot put a price on word-of-mouth marketing.

8. Get a business coach

When you are overwhelmed, unsure, have lost focus, or aren't certain about your mission, find a business coach for objectivity and guidance. A business coach is there to provide you with guidance, bounce ideas off, offer impartial advice and help you to regain focus.

Check out Milton's video '7 Reasons Why You Need a Business Coach' at **deanpublishing.com/ smallsurprises**

"It's good to have money and the things that money can buy, but it's good, too, to check up once in a while and make sure that you haven't lost the things that money can't buy."

— George Lorimer

PAIN POINT #3: TEAM

Whose Job Is It?

This is a little story about four people named Everybody, Somebody, Anybody, and Nobody. There was an important job to be done and Everybody was sure that Somebody would do it. Anybody could have done it, but Nobody did it. Somebody got angry about that because it was Everybody's job.

Everybody thought that Anybody could do it,
but Nobody realised that Everybody wouldn't do it.
It ended up that Everybody blamed Somebody
when Nobody did what Anybody could have done.

Anonymous

ACTIVITY IS NOT ENGAGEMENT

Does *Whose Job Is It* sound familiar? Do you have team problems?

Poor team culture?

Poor leadership?

Lack of initiative?

Lack of bonding?

Poor connection between team members?

A study published in *The Harvard Business Review* stated that "over the past two decades the time spent by managers and employees in collaborative activities has ballooned by 50 percent or more."[32]

Statistically speaking, that means there's going to be more relationship bonds and breakages. More conflicts and collaborations. Therefore, culture is going to be more important than ever, and developing effective team communication skills is now more of a priority than 20 years ago.

In other words, what once worked for teams probably doesn't work anymore. The old system of "I'm the boss" and "you're my staff member" no longer applies in an unbalanced way. Collaboration is the new way; however, it does come with its own new set of challenges that you must be aware of and know how to navigate.

Studies from the McKinsey Global Institute, International Data Corporation, and the *Journal of Communication* show that 50%–80% of the workday is spent in communicating, two-thirds of that in talking.[33]

Now, if you're not a good communicator or you're not being an effective communicator — imagine how damaging your days are? How many disgruntled employees and customers are you unknowingly creating?

On the flipside, imagine the positive impact you could have (or do have) if you are communicating at a high-performance level. If you're solving team pain points and implementing positive cultural changes.

Team pain points can begin in any business, but if you're the business leader — the buck stops with you. You must be able to lead your team in a positive way and make changes to create an incredibly productive and positive work culture. Even if it takes work, you must be willing to make it work.

When I became a CEO or partner in any business, I often found that the team wasn't engaged. I knew it wasn't going to change unless I made it a priority.

Latest figures reflect this too — only 14% of employees in Australia and New Zealand are engaged in their jobs. And a whopping 71% are *not* engaged! As many as 15% are actively disengaged.[34] And it's not only team members in general, but 1 in 5 people in leadership positions are not engaged in their jobs. They don't want to be at work. Across the globe, 85% of employees are not engaged.[35] That's the majority! Now they still may turn up for work, but they're not actively engaged, they're not giving their best.

To break it down, if you're rowing a boat then only a very small portion of employees actually have their oars in the water actively paddling.

14% ENGAGED
KEEPING THINGS RUNNING SMOOTHLY

71% DISENGAGED
ENJOYING THE RIDE

15% ACTIVELY DISENGAGED
MAKING WORK DIFFICULT

ENGAGEMENT IS CRITICAL

It's important to engage with your team and immediately involve them in decision-making. When your team—junior members to senior members—are involved in creating the company vision and goals they often become immediately more engaged. Simply sitting around and doing a vision statement, mission statement or SWOT analysis together can alter the dynamic. Sure, it may sound boring but it sparks communication and direct involvement.

People need to grow and develop with the business, they need to understand what you're trying to achieve. Until the team is together and collectively understands the vision, they won't get ready to set things like goals or Key Performance Indicators (KPIs). In fact, more often than not, I ask members to help set their own KPIs to involve them even deeper into the outcomes and strategies.

Explaining and setting the business philosophy can change the whole team's attitude. Setting visions, looking at the long-term, growing as a team — these are all key factors for creating a high-performance team. Your team are your allies and co-creators.

A great leader has the attitude of 'I want to learn from you too'. The bottom line is, if you're not making team and collaboration a priority — you'll run into a massive amount of problems. But don't worry, in the following chapters, we will go through all the steps to create a high-performance team.

Get your free KPI worksheet at **deanpublishing.com/smallsurprises**

TROUBLESHOOTING THE PAIN POINTS OF YOUR CLIENTS

If you want to *Delight, Disrupt and Deliver* in your industry — you need to know how to effectively deal with pain points.

I use the HEAL Method with solving pain points.

H **HOW**
How will you or your business product or service solve a pain point for people?

E **EVALUATE AND ENGAGE**
What do you require to ensure these pain points are fulfilled? How can you engage people into making this happen?

A **AWARENESS, ASK AND ATTITUDE**
Be aware of what is important to your client. Find out by asking and paying attention to their attitude and feedback.

L **LISTEN AND LEARN**
Be quiet and listen. You won't learn anything new by talking, but you may by listening.

H = HOW

What pain point are you solving for people?

....

....

....

....

....

How can you solve customers' pain points?

....

....

....

....

....

How can you solve your pain points?

....

....

....

....

....

How can you solve your team's pain points?

....

....

....

....

....

E = EVALUATE AND ENGAGE

Evaluate: You need to test and measure everything. Are your systems effective? Do they serve your business as well as your customers? Are there better ways to do things?

If you're not testing and measuring — you're missing out on vital business clues. You need to know what's working and what's not. You can't solve problems if you don't understand your customers' needs.

Once you evaluate your customers' needs you need to evaluate if you have systems and services which support their needs. If not, can you implement them? Evaluate all the pain points you can think of and find ways to solve them.

How can you engage your team to ensure these pain points are addressed?

Engage: Include your team. Ask them to be problem solvers. Engagement increases their productivity and increases their enjoyment in what they're doing. That's really important.

If your team is having fun, the clients will see that and enjoy the environment. Quite often, our teams would make problem-solving a game at work. We'd see how far we could go to please a client.

A = AWARENESS, ASK AND ATTITUDE

Aware: Be aware of your clients' or team's pain points.
Ask: Open the communication channels and ask open-ended questions.
Attitude: Adopt a solution-focused attitude.

If you're not aware and attuned to your clients and you're taking too much time communicate, then things will break down. You must always stay in touch with your team and clients and never stop asking good questions. But don't borderline on interrogation! No one likes a pushy salesperson.

Ask them open-ended questions and *let them talk*. Don't ask simple yes or no questions. Keep digging deeper in a nice way to find out what's important to them. How do they make decisions?

Remember: you're not just trying to sell them a service, you're trying to offer them solutions. If you adopt a solution-orientated attitude to solving their problems, you often get the sale by default anyway — and if you don't — they'll be sure to recommend you to another client for your impeccable service and non-salesy approach.

Have you ever been to Bunnings and asked for assistance? The staff often give you really good advice about how to paint your home or which shelving bracket you need to keep a heavy load off the ground. They offer solutions first. This is the approach. It's not to make your product squeeze into something they don't want or need. It's all in the right approach and adding some care-factor!

L = LISTEN AND LEARN

I personally spend a lot of my time finding out what's happening in the business, listening to my team and learning from our clients. I learn more this way.

Have you ever watched an episode of *Undercover Boss* on TV? It's a show where the boss of a big company (whom most employees have rarely actually met) is heavily disguised, often wearing wigs, different clothing and an entirely different look. They go undercover in their own business and liaise with their staff who believe they are trainees or someone else other than the boss. What's interesting about this show is that the boss often discovers what business is really like and the common problems his or her team really have. It's often a surprise for both the employees and the boss!

This TV show reveals the truth in business, which is — you must understand your business from all ends of the spectrum. From staff, to customers, to industry. And you do this by asking questions and listening. Through listening — you learn.

Radio and TV personality Larry King knew the secret that made him a famous media interviewer. Although he got paid to speak for a living, it was his listening skills that gave him the edge. He said, "I remind myself every morning: Nothing I say this day will teach me anything. So if I'm going to learn, I must do it by listening." Take this approach.

I am always asking my team questions. What was today like?

Was it busy? Was it quiet? Any ideas that you have? What else do you think is critical? What don't you like? What sort of feedback are you getting? What are people saying to you? What are the customers saying? Are they happy?

I have learnt so much about business through this communication process. Plus the team can talk openly and tell me the problems we are having, it builds great rapport and makes them feel important in their jobs too, because they are.

I have found time and time again, that few listen as well as they talk.

SOLUTIONS

When you hear of any issues that arise it's important to be solution-orientated. When I talk to some of my coaching clients, I ask them what their current issues in business are. And they'll often reply, "What do you mean?"

So I'll say, "Well, what worries you? What would you like to improve? If you could do anything tomorrow with your business, what would be the first? Make more money? Get more staff? Buy better equipment?"

Most likely they will share "We can't charge more, or, there isn't a margin in this product, or people aren't paying on time."

They start to bring up things and as they do I keep asking, how do you feel about that, or what have you tried in the past to improve that?

We keep focusing on solutions. It's all about them, and I am here to help them find workable solutions to their problems.

After digging deeper and discovering their pain points, we summarise the list to make it ultra-clear. Offer them solutions and ask them for some of theirs. Find out what they think.

For the best solutions:
- you have to listen to learn
- provide solutions and ask for feedback
- get people to make the final decision themselves but lead them in the right direction
- take immediate focused action when they make their decision
- build on the momentum.

⚜ ⚜

PART TWO

TEAM
FOUNDATIONS

"Business is all about people."

Brad Sugars

———

6 WINNING PRINCIPLES

TO BUILDING A TEAM THAT DELIGHTS, DISRUPTS AND DELIVERS

My *Delight, Disrupt and Deliver* mantra applies to all principles of business, not just to your industry or clients. Of course, you want to delight your clients, disrupt the industry and deliver the best service in your industry, but to do that really well you need a team that is aligned with your vision.

I believe that if you delight your team, they'll delight your customers. And not only that, if you delight your team they'll help disrupt and deliver every time.

DELIGHT:

DELIGHT YOUR TEAM AND THEY'LL DELIGHT YOUR CUSTOMERS

It's no secret that happy team members are the most productive and stay with your company longer. Time and time again new research is showing that happy workers create happy and prosperous businesses. Wellness in the workplace has become a very hot topic of recent times, but it simply reveals what we've always known — put people in an environment where they can thrive, and they will.

No one likes a toxic culture and no one grows well in a toxic culture, much like plants don't grow in an environment of toxins, neither do we.

> *"Clients don't come first — employees come first. If you take care of your employees, they will take care of the clients."*
>
> — *Richard Branson*

DISRUPT:

ENCOURAGE POSITIVE DISRUPTION

Now when I use the word 'disrupt' some business owners scoff, they believe that they're too small to be disruptive in their industry. But disruptive isn't about being the biggest, it's about doing business a different way, finding a gap in the market or changing the way the industry 'has always done it'.

Let me explain. For those who remember life before the internet, encyclopedias were huge investments. You had to pay a lot of money for a collection of encyclopedias. They were produced for profit and printed very thick and heavy, often with gold embossing and regal covers. Fast-forward to today's world and it's hard to find someone who orders a bookshelf full of encyclopedias. Why? Because the world has changed. Encyclopedia Britannica published its final volumes in 2012. To give you some perspective on the significance of this fact, that means after 244 years of print – the 2012 editions of 32 volumes were the last! The world changed rapidly. Fast enough to make one of the oldest and most respected companies in the world, course-correct at rapid speed.

Now, futuristic online companies didn't go out thinking, 'Hey, let's knock over these encyclopedia companies', they simply saw a better way of doing it. A more user-friendly and cheaper alternative. A faster and smarter way. Simple.

Disruptors look for new ways to do business. They often share a common goal to create better products or services, or to innovate existing products or services in a better, more creative, quicker, user-friendly way.

Harvard Business School professor, the late Clayton Christensen is commonly known in business sectors as the guru for disruptive innovation. He even built an entire institute dedicated to disruption — The Clayton Christensen Institute[36], a non-profit organisation dedicated to improving the world through Disruptive Innovation.

Clayton Christensen says that a disruption **displaces an existing market and produces something new and more efficient and worthwhile.**[37]

His theory is that big, powerful companies that overlook or neglect potential customers at the lower end of their markets are sitting ducks for disruption from smaller, more efficient competitors.

In fact, independent research in a different field — (of science and technology) show his theory is correct. One group of researchers analysed more than 65 million papers, patents and software products between the years 1954–2014. They found that "smaller teams have tended to disrupt science and technology with new ideas and opportunities, whereas larger teams have tended to develop existing ones.

Work from larger teams builds on more-recent and popular developments, and attention to their work comes immediately. By contrast, contributions by smaller teams search more deeply into the past, are viewed as disruptive to science and technology and succeed further into the future."[38]

So, it's not the size of the company that matters but the ability to think and act differently. Small teams are the biggest disruptors.

So, encourage your team to ask: what does society need? What do customers want but have difficulty obtaining? Empower your team to come up with new and innovative ways to satisfy your customers or potential clients.

"Never doubt that a small group of thoughtful, committed citizens can change the world; indeed, it's the only thing that ever has."

— *Margaret Mead*

DELIVER:

ALWAYS DELIVER

I mentioned earlier that good businesses promote team members to use their best strengths, to work in their zone of genius. People always function best when they love what they do and get the chance to do it well. When a company delivers — customers are happy. As the saying goes, "Be so good they can't ignore you".

When you use the strength of your team — the entire company thrives. A Gallup study showed that teams that focus on strengths every day have 12.5% higher productivity. The same Gallup analysis reveals that people who use their strengths every day are less stressed and three times more likely to report having an excellent quality of life. They are more engaged at work and 15% less likely to quit their jobs.[39] This makes companies — DELIVER. Well, and often.

Building a team like this has other exciting results. Take the results of one large retailer who was having difficulty providing great customer service to its clients. The company decided to train its employees in how to offer their shoppers good advice and personalised knowledge about their products, installations and repairs.

When the employees were also encouraged to use their strengths, they did an even better job of connecting with customers and providing personalised service. The fascinating result is that the stores which implemented the customer strategy *with* a the strengths-based focus grew 66% faster than stores that didn't add the strengths-based focus.[40]

Could you imagine a 66% growth in your business? How would this alter your ability to deliver? They did all this simply using the team's strengths and encouraging them to flaunt them.

Now to deliver doesn't only mean to give your customers your product or service on time. That's standard. That's average. You've probably heard of the business mantra 'under promise and over deliver'. This is a good mindset to have of course but how many companies actually deliver?! Many 'over promise and under deliver' and this leaves people angry, disappointed and upset. And where do they like to direct those feelings? To anyone and everyone that will listen. Usually on social media when you have thousands of bored people just ready to pounce on any little piece of drama.

I often remind people:
- **DON'T just deliver a product or service**
- **DELIVER an experience**
- **DELIVER a memorable experience**
- **DELIVER a stunning experience**

Over the course of my life, I have used the same principles to help teams Delight, Disrupt and Deliver the best in their industry.

Brad Sugars from ActionCOACH® succinctly identifies six winning principles, and I'd like to share my understanding of these six principles.[41]

6 WINNING PRINCIPLES

TO A HIGH-PERFORMANCE (AND HAPPY) TEAM

1. Sound Leadership
2. A Shared Goal
3. Rules of the Game
4. Action Plan
5. Support Risk-taking
6. 100% Inclusion

"Customers will never love a company until the employees love it first."

— *Simon Sinek*

PRINCIPLE #1: SOUND LEADERSHIP

The most important thing in any business, whether new or established is strong leadership. A ship doesn't sail without a captain and an aeroplane does not take to the air without a pilot. They essentially are the leaders of their crew. They don't do all the jobs, but they navigate the direction and make strong decisions on behalf of everyone. Businesses require the same leadership.

Without sound leadership, it's very difficult to develop a thriving team culture. There needs to be someone who has got the right emotion, the right intention, and the right vision. There must be someone capable enough to develop the team in a way that is conducive to help everyone flourish. It's someone who shows rather than tells. That's a really important fact. If you can't help your team develop and grow, you're not the leader.

Personally, I love to hire people that are much smarter than I am. When I'm selecting someone, I want people who are better at that role than I am, then they can develop and use their skills to a higher limit and benefit everyone. But you've got to give them permission to do that. So, true leadership is actually helping others bring out the best in themselves.

Richard Branson is a master of this craft. What has made him so successful is the fact he has broken the rules of what was once considered 'leadership'. He admits he is a rule-breaker, but says it's because he never learnt the rules in the first place. He actively encourages every employee to become an innovative thinker and gives them permission to add their unique personality and value to the company in their own way.

He says, "my number one rule in business, and in life, is to enjoy what you do. Running a business involves long hours and hard decisions;

if you don't have the passion to keep you going, your business will more than likely fail. If you don't enjoy what you are doing, then you shouldn't be doing it."

Branson defined the "new way of doing business". That fun, laughter, hard decisions and passion and good leadership can all go hand-in-hand together. I believe this way is the only way. That the old leadership style of "I tell and you do" is ineffective. The new style of leadership is "I show, we do". Which, if you develop your team members into leaders, will become "we show, we do".

As Reid Hoffman, LinkedIn cofounder says, "No matter how brilliant your mind or strategy, if you're playing a solo game, you'll always lose out to a team."

When I was President of a BNI® chapter, I came across Graham Weihmiller, Chairman and CEO of BNI®, who wrote a great article about leadership.[42] BNI are passionate to grow more strong and thoughtful leaders and expand their mission of Changing the Way the World Does Business®. Not to mention their Core Value, Givers Gain® — meaning the more you give, the more you receive.

Here are five leadership qualities Graham recommends for leaders to consider.

- **Leaders can take criticism** — In fact, leaders welcome other viewpoints. No matter what, at some point in your career you will be criticized. But it's what you do with that criticism that will define you. Will you listen? Will you try to understand varying perspectives? True leaders can take criticism, and turn their setbacks into success.

- **Leaders maintain a positive attitude** — Your attitude is infectious. Both in and out of the workplace, leaders speak with compassion and kindness no matter the circumstances.

- **Leaders praise others' achievements** — Equally important to your success is the success of those around you. Effective leaders understand this, and truly enjoy celebrating the accomplishments of their peers and teams.

- **Leaders treat others the way they'd like to be treated** — By this I mean they are flexible and adaptable. Think about what motivates others around you, and the varying working styles your team may have. True leaders can identify these preferences, and adapt their leadership style accordingly.
- **Leaders learn from their mistakes** — You will make mistakes, and that's okay. But accountability is essential. Take responsibility. Identify what you could do differently next time. Share what you learned with others, so they too can learn from your mistakes.

PRINCIPLE #2: A SHARED GOAL TO PURSUE

To make this point I'd like to share a story commonly shared in many cultures, often with some little differences.

> *A New York businessman was sitting on the beach on a small island. He was having a holiday and watching people fish nearby. A small-framed fisherman was rowing a tiny boat towards the shore. He had caught an impressive number of big fish and looked happy with himself.*
>
> *The businessman yelled over the water to the man, "Good catch!"*
>
> *The fisherman smiled wide.*
>
> *When the fisherman came to shore the businessman went over to check out his fishing secrets. They discussed today's catch and the fisherman was excited to take dinner home to his wife and numerous kids.*
>
> *The business man was a very wealthy man and thought it may be nice to help the fisherman. He could tell by his clothes and lifestyle that he wasn't very rich.*
>
> *"Listen" said the businessman. "I have a successful company and a PhD in economics. Why don't you fish a bit more, then hire a*

few young men, put some more boats on the water and get more fish. Make a profit off each boat. You'd make a fortune."

The fisherman looked puzzled, "Then what do I do?"

"Then you can buy a nice big house, get some bigger boats and get more fish."

The fisherman asked, "then what do I do?"

"Then one day you can sell everything and retire rich."

"Then what do I do?" asked the fisherman.

"Then you can spend your days doing whatever you want."

"Like fishing for a few hours and then spending the rest of my time with my family?" he asked.

"Exactly" said the businessman proudly.

"That's what I am already doing," smiled the fisherman as he flipped the fish over his shoulder and headed off home. "Maybe I'm rich already."

There are quite a few morals within this story, one is on the definition of "success" and another is about goals. Know your goals without becoming blindsided to why you want to achieve them.

The team needs to have a shared goal so everyone can become enrolled in the vision and inspire each other. There must be a shared vision and common goals to work towards. Otherwise you have a group of business people and a group of fishermen or women — driven by different motivations.

It's also important to look behind the goal and assess your intention and emotion around the goal. Does the common goal have a good and noble intention? Is there a level of positive emotion around it?

If people just fake smile and nod when you talk about company goals, the bottom line is: the goal isn't good enough. Goals should arouse emotion and excitement, they should ignite action and have a purpose deeper than just making money.

I believe it's imperative to involve the team in decision making, to work through the vision of the business so everyone can take ownership of it. Doing things like a group SWOT analysis to look at ways to improve is a good example. Asking everyone — what are our strengths and weaknesses? Where can we improve?

STRENGTHS	WEAKNESSES	OPPORTUNITIES	THREATS
1.	1.	1.	1.
2.	2.	2.	2.
3.	3.	3.	3.

S W O T

Goals and culture go hand-in-hand. If you bring everyone together and you set your goals and vision as one, it's already establishing a better culture. The goal and vision shouldn't be something that the boss has dreamed up. Personally, I hate the word 'boss' because that's not what it should be, it should be leader, not boss. I'm also not a fan of using the word 'staff', I like to talk about a team. As one person, you're not going to do a hell of a lot, but as you a team you can really achieve so much more. As Henry Ford said, "Coming together is a beginning, staying together is progress, and working together is success."

Here's the truth — you can't expect your team to achieve a goal that they don't know about or feel included in. According to Workboard, 69% of high-performing companies said that communicating their business goals was the leading tool for creating a high-performance team.[43]

Download your free SWOT plan at **deanpublishing. com/smallsurprises**

PRINCIPLE #3: RULES OF THE GAME

You can't play the most strategic game of chess if you don't know the rules of the game. You'll get check-mated by your opponent (who knows the rules) quicker than you can swallow your pride. To build an incredible, thriving team of achievers, you've got to know the standards and norms. You've got to know things like:

- What's acceptable in your work culture and what's not
- How you need to behave as a team
- What results are expected in your industry
- How will you achieve those goals together

I often start with the basics, like turning up on time and dressing appropriately. It's important that everyone knows the expectations upfront. Also, having respect for each other, outlining the culture of what's expected — like listening and not blaming. Set the standards from the start and keep them raised.

Now, if you're stepping into a new role where the previous culture was set poorly, some people won't come along with you. Some will love it but others won't be capable, or may not have the attitude to embrace a new culture. If they drop off, that's fine too, because a high-performance attitude doesn't suit everybody. You've got to have people with the right attitude that want to grow and develop together and grow the business.

Those who aren't prepared to do that, the team won't tolerate. You need to have the right culture. It's important the culture is refined so people really want to live by it.

Now the Rules of the Game aren't a strict code like a monastery, often when people know the rules, or expectations, they can relax because they don't have to think of everything themselves. The rules of the game shows your team that there is support and training, that they don't have to be fully responsible for everything. A good set of rules supports risk taking and encourages personality without compromising company standards.

You can set **Rules of the Game** for things like:
- interaction with clients
- answering the phone
- workplace manners
- positive attitude markers such as smiling or saying thank you
- communicating with team members
- etiquette for emailing customers
- cleaning of the premises
- uniforms
- health and safety in the workplace.

This doesn't mean you thump down a *War and Peace* style workbook with a long list of rules to abide by, it means you develop codes of conduct together and make each other accountable in implementing them.

The other thing that helps is what I like to call Positional Contracts. Now, Positional Contracts are about what that particular position in the firm is, it's not about the individual, it's the job role. It's important to develop a system so when a person moves on or the business changes, you have got that position clearly defined with its roles and responsibilities.

Again, you can ask your team members to help develop it, and it's often much better if they do because they clearly define the roles within the broader business system and understand what's needed for growth. There's also certain things in that positional contract that need to happen.

If a new person doesn't have the necessary skills for example, they need to be trained or it needs to be given to an appropriate candidate. This makes the team really, really effective.

System manuals and process manuals are also fantastic tools so people can be trained well and know the Rules of the Game within your business. System manuals aren't meant to be static documents that never change, they should be a growing, live and dynamic document that evolves as your business grows.

PRINCIPLE #4: ACTION PLAN

To have a winning team, you have got to have an action plan. The action plan can be really simple, it can be, who is going to do something, what they're going to do, and by when.

Who — What — When

That's how I love to run meetings, I don't like big long meetings, I just like a strong action plan. I think that one person needs to take responsibility for each action, and they can delegate those actions but they inevitably remain responsible for actioning that plan.

It can be a good idea to use an action plan template to record who is responsible for doing an action and by when.

MY AMAZING COMPANY'S ACTION PLAN

GOAL	TASKS	SUCCESS CRITERIA	TIME FRAME	RESOURCES
(What are the team objectives)	(What tasks need to be done to achieve the goals)	(How will success be identified)	(When does the task need to achieved by)	(What you will need for each task)

To get your FREE download 'Action Plan Template', go to **deanpublishing.com/smallsurprises**

PRINCIPLE #5: SUPPORT RISK TAKING

"Come to the edge," he said. "We can't, we're afraid!" they responded. "Come to the edge," he said. "We can't, We will fall!" they responded. "Come to the edge," he said. And so they came. And he pushed them. And they flew.

— *Guillaume Apollinaire*

I love to be able to empower team members to use their wings and fly, to actively look for and seek out new ideas and opportunities. If you don't look for breakthroughs, how can you expect one?

Ask everyone:
- *How else can we improve that?*
- *What else can we do that's brave, or different?*
- *What is something new we can try?*

Businesses need to be growing all the time, if you're not growing, you're either stagnating or regressing. If you're not progressing, your competitors will be. The good ones are growing all the time and improving what they do and how they do it.

But to be leading-edge, it's all about developing relationships. It's relationships within your own team, and of course with your customers and your clients. Relationship building is critical in order to support risk-taking in business. If everyone is on-board and willing to go that extra mile in doing something different, then the risk is more likely to pay off.

Change can make or break some companies. But change is inevitable. The art form is changing and progressing positively.

The Japanese have a word for it, *Kaizen*, which is constant and never-ending improvement.

KAI
Change

ZEN
Good

改 善

KAIZEN = Continuous Improvement

I think Kaizen is a fantastic philosophy because you need to be developing and creating enthusiasm about change. Now, of course, you might plateau for a while, then you might grow again, and then plateau. That's normal too, because you're adapting and developing at every new stage. Being willing to change and innovate is critical for success.

In a recent McKinsey poll, 84% of global executives reported that innovation was extremely important to their growth strategies, but a staggering 94% were dissatisfied with their organisation's innovation performance.[44]

But when I read that statistic I couldn't help but wonder, how many people felt supported to innovate and take risks? Was the whole team trained in undertaking this new change?

Innovation and risk-taking is wonderful but it must be supported by your team members for it to be a true success. When you think about it clearly, business development and entrepreneurship is fundamentally linked to risk-taking. It often begins with a risk. But taking a well-thought-out risk with team support is very different to taking a gamble-style risk and hope it lands on your lucky number. One is planned and considers the options, the other is a stab in the dark at a moving target.

The most important factor for risk-taking is that there's some room in your business for it. That there is mental space for exploring new horizons and considering new ways to do things.

When we owned Campaspe Country House, there were certain things I liked in hospitality, but there was one thing I have always hated — that is, buffets. I think buffets are dreadful. I even hate the word. I think it brings out the worst in people too. I don't like food just sitting on a table, getting spoiled and dry.

It may look great when the first guest sees it, but when they're halfway through it looks like a dog's breakfast. So, we used to say we're a "buffet free zone". Now, we'd have people come in, and they'll say they want a buffet for their event, be it a wedding, party or business function. We would smile and say, "We're a buffet-free zone, we don't do buffets."

The guests would look shocked. And then we would say, "We do wandering feasts". It was a term I came up with that stirred the imagination and ignited curiosity. Wandering feasts are a glorified cocktail party but with fabulous fresh foods, straight from the kitchen. It would allow people to stand outside or move around and we would serve them a fresh wandering feast.

We did many amazing wandering feasts, we'd do it for weddings, for birthday parties or commercial get togethers or conference groups. People loved it. The food was more substantial than cocktail food and totally fresh, unlike a buffet.

Now, it was a risk at the time being a "buffet-free zone" but we didn't just stomp our feet and sook about buffets, we offered a better alternative. We made a name for ourselves, because no one else used that term. We didn't even know the term wandering feast, but we thought about it and we loved it. To me it was fabulous, and it worked.

PRINCIPLE #6: 100% INVOLVEMENT & INCLUSION

Developing a positive and inclusive synergy with your team is imperative. A great business is a place where everyone is encouraged to give ideas, to be involved with the team and team decisions. Teams need to know how to perform together.

One classic example is the 1992 US men's Olympic basketball team, called "The Dream Team". It had some of the greatest players in the history of the sport all in one team, people like Charles Barkley, Larry Bird, Patrick Ewing, Magic Johnson, Michael Jordan and Scottie Pippen.

Just heaping these players together in one team didn't guarantee success. In fact, during their first month of training, the "Dream Team" lost to a group of college players by eight points in a scrimmage. Scottie Pippen summed it up perfectly when he said, "We didn't know how to play with each other." They humbly learned how to play as one unit, and the rest is history. The team not only won the 1992 Olympic gold medal but also dominated the competition, scoring over 100 points in every game. Luckily, they learned to make room for each other, to not be great alone but great together.

If there's a problem, don't blame individuals, talk about how the team or the system could be improved. For example, rather than saying, "I can't get the invoices from Tom and get the delivery to happen on time." We need to be able to say, "How can we improve our system so the documents come back faster and we get the invoices?"

Ask the team — How do we do that? So, it's not about Tom, it's how we improve the overall system.

I think it's much better synergy with the team, it creates respect for each other, but also it allows you to work on a system to improve it for your customers' benefit.

Before I first joined the Transport Hotel Group, there was Taxi Kitchen and all the other restaurants and bars there. I went along to the restaurant before anyone there knew who I was. I went there as a mystery diner. I went along with my wife and two teenage children. We dined in the restaurant and had a drink in the bar.

At the end of the dining experience, we each made a list of all things that needed improvement; unfortunately, it was quite a long list at the time. There was a lack of atmosphere and warmth, we really were treated like a number, not a welcomed guest.

The front door greeting was almost an interrogation, "Hey, have you got a booking and what's it under?" Then the person on the front desk rushed off with a menu in her hand and basically left us behind. She was at our table as we were standing halfway across the restaurant. She dropped the menu on the table and started walking back passing us halfway back to the table. It was stonecold 'service'.

It was really good to be able to see that from the start. As we dined some major things became apparent and I said to my family, "This is good because there's so much room for improvement."

I knew from one dinner that we had to change the culture and attitudes first. I could clearly see that the team needed better training and engagement. In a strange way, I became very excited because the potential was there and I knew we could turn it around.

The week before I officially started my role, I organised to meet all the senior people in the team. I made sure that I got a breakdown of all the team names, positions and roles so I knew a little bit about them, their department and their role beforehand. I also knew how long they had been with the company and a bit of their previous background. We had a morning tea together. I just wanted to talk to them and find out more about them. I asked lots of questions about their roles, their goals, and what they felt needed to be improved.

Now that really impressed them. They were surprised that I knew things about them before we had met. But it was really simple, it was only some information about their names, their roles and previous experience. But they felt comfortable that I had done my research, and wanted to know about them. Once again it was about them, not about me.

So I was asking them what they liked about their job, what they'd like to change, what they thought might be able to improve in the business. What else was needed in the business to help it grow and develop. Did they have any other ideas? I didn't want to discuss it all at our first meeting but I asked them to think about it for the future, as we work together as a team, and I really explained it was all about being a team. I explained to them that I wasn't coming in as a new boss, I was coming in as one of them.

Yes, I wanted to provide leadership. Yes, I wanted to give them some good common goals and a vision, but I wanted them to know that it wasn't about being a boss, it was about us working as a team. It was about 100% inclusion.

I quickly realised that they never had team meetings, they didn't have a vision or goals. So, all that soon changed.

With their insight and input and some strong leadership and training, things changed. Things changed for the better — and quickly. It was quite extraordinary.

Good leadership is not telling people what to do but providing good direction so we can all move forward together. Yes, people still have a job to do, and yes, they've got to do their role well, but it's about asking them how we can all do it better and getting that feedback. Now, some employees will miss the point and some may come up with some strange ideas, but they're not wrong. Their ideas may be impractical or even useless, but it's more about the openness to communicate what we're trying to achieve with the culture of the business. It's about listening and learning. It's about inclusion.

It's also important that as people change, as the business grows, that the team sticks together. Of course, not all people are going to stay forever but the longer they do, the better. If they're good in their role, and they want to grow, but perhaps also want to move up the ladder and gain more responsibility. It becomes super important that you've got the right rituals and culture there. So when new team members come on-board, they can be accepted and understand what's expected. It's critical for people to feel part of the team as quickly as possible.

Sometimes after a big function, our team would sit back and have a debrief, we would ask — what worked out well and where can we improve? Where was the wow factor for our customers? How do we go to the next level?

That not only includes everybody but it inspires the team too. People love to be involved, the question is are you involving your team? Is everyone feeling involved and included? You can be completely diverse and still be fully included. This is where the greatness is.

Boris Groysberg and Katherine Connolly from Harvard Business School conducted a study in 2013 comprising of 24 companies with a steady reputation for having diverse workplaces and making diversity a priority.[45] One of their chief findings was summed up perfectly by Paul Block, the CEO of Merisant who said, "People with different lifestyles and different backgrounds challenge each other more. Diversity creates dissent, and you need that. Without it, you're not going to get any deep inquiry or breakthroughs."[46]

Managers can develop a better understanding of their team by asking them questions and spending time with them exploring the answers. Questions like:

1. *What do you love to do the most?*
2. *What would you like the opportunity to do or explore but haven't done yet?*
3. *What sorts of activities do you finish and think, "I can't wait to do that again"? Or what are you passionate about — inside or outside work?*
4. *What have you done well that you didn't need someone to explain how to do?*
5. *What have other people told you you're great at doing?*
6. *Where would you like extra support or training?*

**Further into this book, the DISC analysis will help you fully understand each learning and personality style and be able to help all team members better so they can use their strengths and operate in their genius zone.

TIPS TO SUPPORT THE 6 WINNING PRINCIPLES

USE THE WIFLE METHOD

As an ActionCOACH® business coach, I was taught a very important principle. One I have since implemented and use multiple times with outstanding results. They call it a WIFLE. Which is an acronym for, *What I Feel Like Expressing.*

A WIFLE is a small amount of time that allows each team member to express what is currently going on in his or her life, both in the business and personally.

Every time we get together as a group, either in webinars or with other coaches that I work with, we do a WIFLE at the start of the meeting. I also use it with all my clients at the start of their coaching session, every fortnight we have a WIFLE session.

It doesn't have to be about work, it's just about what they (or I) feel like expressing, and it might be a personal emotion, it might be some problems at hand, it might be something fantastic, but it should have a positive tone. If you're in a team environment it can be done at a group meeting. You can begin with one person and go around the room one by one.

The person speaking can say whatever he or she feels like saying *without interruption*. This is the most important part. It's *not* a conversation. It's an expression and they must feel safe to say whatever they feel without retribution. Try and keep things respectful and positive. As the leader, you should keep everyone in-check and make sure that everyone gets time to express themselves freely without criticism or judgement. Reiterate that there's nothing right or wrong, it's an exercise of expressing and listening.

TEACH QUESTION SOFTENERS

When building a high-performance team, it's important to use, and train them to use, questions softeners. Questions like:

May I ask?

By the way...

Incidentally,

Can I suggest...

So it softens the questions you are asking and helps people feel more relaxed with answering.

I always find that if you start to ask genuine questions, people love to tell you and talk. People like to talk and that's how they actually sell themselves, because they'll be sharing with you what is important to them, what their issues are, what problems they need to be solved — and then, if your product or service can provide that — you're home and hosed.

Train your team in the art of question softeners. It's a subtle skill but potent in outcomes.

In the hospitality profession, asking people soft questions like, "May I help you with the menu? What types of foods are your favourite?" Some diners will instantly ask, "What's good today?" or "What do you recommend?" This is a great opportunity to ask them what they like to eat. What type of cuisines do they like? Do they like garlic? Break it down and then give them advice rather than just shooting off from the hip and saying, "Oh, the steak is great today." They might be vegetarian for all you know. Find out first what they like. Once again, make it personal to them.

Now, many people assume that these principles only work with a small team but they work with all sized teams. For larger teams, you can break them down into smaller departments and train the managers in implementing them.

At Taxi Kitchen and Hotel, I used to get my managers from each area to sit together, we'd meet once a week, and each of the managers would discuss their issues, their plans and their budgets. They'd do this with their own team and also with each other manager. That way, they all understood the different working parts of the business, they understood what each department was going through, and where they could best help each other. Each manager could work as a cog in a larger wheel and help each other.

Once we broke things down with each manager and their team,we would then either do training days together, or meet on a regular basis. The managers became the ones who filtered any new information orrelevant communication to their team.

The key was communication, it was really important to make sure that everybody gets the vital information that's going through the system too. When dealing with a whole team of leaders, question softeners can really help. They curb any tension and help offer suggestions to each other without fear of judgement or criticism. Once the managers begin to use it with each other, they can then filter this out to their team and begin to implement it into the working culture.

"You manage things; you lead people."

— Grace Hopper

NEVER FORGET FUN AND FAMILY

Sometimes as we desperately try to balance our profit-and-loss statements and organise our business schedules, we forget what's important. We forget the reason why we got into business in the first place. Sometimes we even forget to have fun. Sadly, sometimes people forget to spend time with the ones they love the most.

I'm not preaching here by the way, I have certainly had times when I have 'forgotten' to have fun and have been 'too busy' to arrive home on time.

Someone who seems to do this better than most is Richard Branson. He broke all the so-called conventional rules and made business fun again. He is often seen dressed up in costume or treating his staff to a new experience. He said, "Fun is at the core of the way I like to do business and it has been key to everything I've done from the outset. More than any other element, fun is the secret of Virgin's success."[47]

He goes onto explain that it's certainly not what business school teachers advocate, nor is it conventional, but it certainly is a key element to how he rose, and continues to rise to great heights. And look at what he has achieved, it's all about his team and how he inspires them to grow and have fun.

It's important that you encourage your team to have a life outside of work, play sport or have some hobbies. As a business leader, it's important to remember your team are human, they want to laugh and feel good about their work.

In the past, we have done things like bring in a masseuse to give massages to the team. Or we had golf days or tennis days — where you got to try new things out and bring the whole family along. It can be good to reward the family too, as often team members spend more time at work than they do with their family. So it's a really nice way of saying, "Thank you for sharing your family member with us." Letting them know how much we value their united sacrifice too.

Work life balance is a very big thing at the moment as the world is getting faster and technology is expanding, people feel "on" more than ever. Time out is critical. It helps people recharge and feel positive about coming to work.

Often, we used to take our team on winery tours. I'd take them out on a bus on a Monday, on their day off, and we would go to a wine region. I would line up about four or five wineries to visit (and because we were a prominent restaurant) the wineries were quick to entertain us.

We would always be given a great day at no charge. We'd be given great lunches and great tours around incredible wineries during the time they weren't open to the public. They would let us in and show us around. The team engagement was fantastic and rapport building. They loved what they learned.

Now, these winemakers were also clever. They were showing and educating our team all about their wines. So, can you guess which wine the team really pushed for the next weeks and months? They met the wine makers, they got to meet the owners and gain insight into their wine knowledge and story. They were really proud of their new knowledge of wine and food and it made a huge difference. They were telling our customers about the local regions and sharing incredible knowledge about the winery.

If you take the time to educate and train and build those foundations, training doesn't have to be done over and over again. You don't have to constantly put out all those little fires, you know your team is educated to handle prickly questions.

EVERYONE SHOULD BE GROWING WITHOUT YOU

Everyone in the team should be growing so that the whole place is not reliant on you. The systems must be in place, the teams in place, so then it can grow and develop. You don't have to be there watching it every second.

Which is quite egoless, and where some owners struggle. Some owners feel that they're not needed and some think that the only way a business will grow is with them watching it like a hyperactive hawk.

You need to develop a profitable enterprise that works without you. It's the whole ethos of ActionCOACH® (actioncoach.com), that's what we help our customers build and grow. A commercial, profitable enterprise that can grow and develop with you. That frees you up to look at other opportunities, or to grow the business in a different direction or start another business. Because it's also systemised with the right people in the right place, and the right team — the business also becomes very solid and saleable.

If you can develop the right team, the team will look after your customers. So if you look after your team and develop them, they look after the customers, because they've got systems, they're consistent, they're empowered, they understand the culture, and they understand the common goal. So they look after all your customers. Then if they look after your customers well, your customers look after your business, because they keep coming back, because they're empowered.

HIRE WELL

There is a mantra I use in business — 'hire slow, fire quick'. This means that you should take your time when bringing someone into your company and if it is not working out, let the person go quickly. Though there is some basis for this, I believe that if you try and hire well from the get-go, you'll nail it the first time and rarely have to go through the merry-go-round of the hire-fire-hire-fire process. But of course, this only happens in a perfect world and it's never a perfect world.

For example, if you've got a sales person who you're consistently getting complaints about, find out the problem and either provide support and training to help them change their ways, or move them on if this doesn't work. I personally don't encourage anyone to allow bad business practices to continue. A toxic person can be like a cancer that runs through and infects the life force of the business. Personally, I hire slowly but not everyone has that luxury — so make sure you think about the right person, not just any person.

A Harvard Business School study found that one of the biggest red flag personality traits in an employee is the constant need to spread negativity.[48] Do you know someone like this? You know the type, always has something negative to say, or a complaint to make. Now, don't confuse this with their ability to do their job because the research shows that they could in fact be a star performer in their actual role but their personality is toxic and they love to say negative things about the company, their job or others.

The study involved data on more than 50,000 employees. And interestingly, the details revealed that those who carry this "toxic trait" can cause a lot of widespread damage to a business — things like the loss of customers, reduction in employee morale and conflict with other staff.

In 2019, The Australian Bureau of Statistics estimated that around 1.1 million Australian employees changed employers (or the businesses they ran) and two thirds of those employees left voluntarily. The most common reason for leaving was 'wanting to obtain better job conditions or wanting a change'.[49]

Turnover rates during this time were particularly high in the hospitality, real estate and administrative services. Yet certain industries are harder than others in many respects, for example, hospitality and childcare often have higher turnover rates because many aren't seeing these roles as a long-term career. Some industries have longer hours or night hours and this can impact people's choices.

But it's important to help people achieve their best and get rewarded for that too. It's not just financial rewards, it's about being really proud of what they do.

In the first interview, I often tell a new employee, "If you want an easy job, don't come and work here. Because we are really exact in what we expect. We are always trying to go the next level in everything we do."

I also tell them, "If you want to grow, develop, learn and be part of a team that requests lots of input from you, we are a good fit. But if you *don't* want to be involved in the team, I can give you a list of 10 other places in town that will employ you, because it's far easier, and they don't have our standards. But if you come and work with us, it will be fun, it'll be dynamic, and you'll be respected. To have us on your CV, you'll get a job anywhere. Because the training you will get here and what you learn will be powerful for any career you go into."

The people who want to grow will say, "That's for me".

Some will stare at you blankly, others will be engaged instantly. It's all about attitude, because many skills can be taught.

When I first started at Taxi Kitchen in Melbourne, I noticed a really strange thing. The place relied heavily on backpackers. Now this was a busy 220 seat restaurant and I noticed a lot of the team hadn't been well trained. They didn't have a recruitment policy. All these different people would wander in with a resume and get a job. It was bizarre. Now, I love employing anyone with a good attitude — but how long do you think travelling backpackers stay around for? And how much do they know about local cuisine?

So we decided to change things. Our team asked, "Who is going to be great in this area?" Bingo! The answer was university students. They're smart and probably needing some extra work as they study. Melbourne University was also just down the road from us. The uni has a huge range of residents that can get to work easily. They'll probably want two or three shifts a week at minimum, and then holidays of course, when we're busy around Christmas time, they'll probably want full-time work. So we started that recruitment process and got quite a few students from Melbourne University. They were fantastic. They were quick to learn, reliable and open to growth. And they needed the money, of course. They're students. All students need money.

When I first spoke to them, I said, "This is not a quick fill-in job. We'll give you great skills that you'll be able to use in life. It's not just being a waiter. You'll learn a huge range of customer service skills. We'll help you build other experience too, and as a prominent restaurant in Melbourne, we'll look good on your CV. And if you stay with us, we'll promote you too. You'll see other leadership roles available."

That worked well for us. We provided the right training. We put a full procedure in place that was all well documented so everyone knew, "This is how we do things at Taxi".

GET A COACH AND PROVIDE MENTORS

Any time a new team member is hired, I love to put them with a mentor or someone to work with them. They need a go-to person. It might be someone who works alongside them or someone senior to them.

A mentor helps new members understand what's acceptable and what's not. Yes, it should be in your systems manual, but nothing beats face-to-face learning and understanding. Manuals can be overwhelming whereas people can 'show' you what to do and support you with emotion and understanding.

Different people learn in different ways. Some people are auditory, they like to listen and that's how they learn. Other people are much more visual, they need to see things, diagrams, see how things operate to learn better. Others need to be shown and experience it, kinaesthetic.

Having a mentor helps new members understand the rules of the game. A mentor can understand what motivates them, how they handle tasks and provide them with great support and encouragement. But mentors and coaches aren't just for new people. I often coach very established business owners who are looking to grow or increase their turnover.

I believe in coaching. Just like professional sportspeople have coaches, I believe business people should also have a business coach. You need to get the edge and the best way to do that is to learn from people who have done what you want to do. As the saying goes "success leaves clues".

I love horse-riding. In fact, for many years my passion was to be a good rider, but I wasn't very talented. I had to work really hard at it. It didn't come naturally. There were other people with more natural skills than me. I had to work hard toward becoming a good rider, but to do this, I made sure I had good coaches. I had really great coaches that helped me develop and grow.

This wasn't just an odd coaching session here or there, I had them throughout the year, year after year. I had a dressage coach; a show jumping coach; a cross country coach, and even a visiting instructor from overseas. I spent a lot of time being coached and it made all the difference!

Without those coaches, I wouldn't have been able to grow and compete against the top riders in Australia. Yes, I had to work damn hard for it but those coaches kept me on track and kept the pressure on, they helped me set goals and improve on a weekly basis, and in the longer term too.

Sometimes coaches aren't just for improvements, they are about accountability, to ensure you get it done.

I also used to sit with my coaches and ask, "Okay, what are we going to achieve in the next eight months?" They all said to me, "Our other students never do that." I said, "But I want to know where I'm going. I've got to have a goal or I can't do it. I need something to aim for. That's what motivates me. I personally can't go and ride my horse every day, I'd get bored. I need to know where I'm heading."

The same method applied in business. It's the same for anything. Music tutors, football coaches, singing teachers, Sous chefs, personal trainers. The list goes on. A good coach can lead you toward success but you have to do the walking.

WHAT'S POSSIBLE IN LESS THAN A YEAR?

Senior leaders from the McKinsey Group, Scott Keller and Mary Meaney, work with corporations and world-class business leaders around leadership. In a McKinsey article they said, "In our experience, those who make a concerted effort to build a high-performing team can do so well within a year, even when starting from a low base."[50]

Let me say that again: You can turn your entire team around in less than one year even if you're starting from scratch!

This has been my experience too. With the right leadership, strategies and attitude — you can have a high-performance team.

In fact, this is the very reason that I coach people for a year or more. So they can be encouraged and nursed through the entire transition. So they can go from a low-performing team to an active and engaged high-performing team in mere months. It's a commitment to change but the rewards are worth it. Well worth it.

TEAM MOTIVATION

A lot of people ask me, "How do you get an entire team motivated?" The bottom-line is if you haven't got the first six principles of a high-performing team in place, you can't expect people to feel continually motivated.

Let's audit ourselves first and go through a general list:

6 PRINCIPLES TO BUILDING GREAT TEAMS

Mark yourself from 1-10 (1 being poor and 10 being excellent).

Principle 1: Strong Leadership
Are you leading the way?

1	2	3	4	5	6	7	8	9	10

Principle 2: A Common Goal
Does everyone on the team know the vision, mission and goals of the team?

1	2	3	4	5	6	7	8	9	10

Are you all pursuing a common goal?

1	2	3	4	5	6	7	8	9	10

Principle 3: Rules of the Game
Have you clearly outlined the rules and expectations of each role and department?

1	2	3	4	5	6	7	8	9	10

Do you have systems and manuals in place?

1	2	3	4	5	6	7	8	9	10

Principle 4: Action Plan

Is there a clear daily and weekly action plan? Do you know who is doing what and when?

1	2	3	4	5	6	7	8	9	10

Is there an action plan in place for 6 months, one year, 5 years?

1	2	3	4	5	6	7	8	9	10

Principle 5: Support Risk Taking

Does the working culture support new ideas, fresh innovative thinking and risk taking?

1	2	3	4	5	6	7	8	9	10

Are you making deliberate time for brainstorming and thinking outside the box?

1	2	3	4	5	6	7	8	9	10

Principle 6: 100% Inclusion

Is everyone included in the business?

1	2	3	4	5	6	7	8	9	10

Are you working your team's strengths and providing regular opportunities for engagement?

1	2	3	4	5	6	7	8	9	10

SCORE: ....

MOTIVATION MATTERS: WAYS TO DELIGHT YOUR TEAM

ENVIRONMENT MATTERS

When people are engaged and enjoying what they're doing, and when smiles and laughter radiates through a room — it's infectious. A positive environment is infectious. Whereas if people are glum and no one is happy, you don't want to be there as a customer.

Every person, whether guest or team member wants to feel comfortable walking into your work environment. To me, the most important thing in any business is a warm and welcoming environment, because it's always awkward walking into a room. Even if you know the place well, that arrival is always the worst part. It's important to be welcomed. To be made to feel comfortable.

Do you have a warm reception? A welcoming environment. Have a scan of your direct environment. It is welcoming?

And for your team, does it encourage motivation? Does it help your team do their job seamlessly? Do you have the right equipment and facilities? Are they well trained to do their job properly? Is your inspiring business vision on the wall? Do you have some nice plants and décor?

A 2011 study from a group of world class researchers showed that a poor work environment can impact workers' moods. In the study, workers in older buildings with low ceilings and loud air conditioners were far more stressed than those in newer buildings with more natural light and spacious, open layouts.[51]

Now of course, that doesn't mean you should go out and purchase an entire new building to keep employees happy. A mechanic shop can't avoid the smell of oil for example. But perhaps looks at ways you can make it a better place to be.

Are you providing an environment that makes them feel proud of their job? It all begins with how everyone feels.

Walk around and talk with your team, find out about them. Make it comfortable for them to approach you. It could simply be a small chat in the morning or a chat near the water cooler or coffee machine. But that's really important, especially the higher up in the leadership role you are. Make some notes and know who their partners are, if they've got children or not. Where they like to holiday. Are they into sport? Which sports team do they barrack for? Treat your team as people not money makers for your company.

One good example of this is Jim Senegal, CEO of Costco. He has a reputation for taking great care of his employees. He pays them well and provides them with health care benefits. He's often seen helping the employees stack shelves or answer phones. He spends time with his employees asking them about their needs and wants. The results speak for themselves — he has a loyal crew and a low staff turnover rate. Often five times lower than his competitors.

He says, "It's really pretty simple. It's good business. When you hire good people, and you provide good jobs and good wages and a career, good things are going to happen."[52] He also says, "People are happy with a job for more reasons than money. There's generally a pride in the organisation...There's an attitude that there's security, that somebody does care about them, that we're offering careers. We're not offering jobs; we're offering careers."[53]

Each year Statista and Forbes survey 30,000 workers to determine the best employer. Costco has consistently appeared in the top three, so it's obvious they are providing something special. They are providing careers within a happy work environment.

See Milton's video about how to work as a high-performance team at **deanpublishing.com/smallsurprises**

BE FLEXIBLE, NOT FIXED

Workplaces have changed a lot in the last 20 years. Working 9–5 isn't the common thing any more. Flexibility is paramount to adapt to these changing environments.

Check if it's possible to offer more flexibility or remote working opportunities. When you can achieve a more balanced work approach you get happy employees and higher productivity.

Allow autonomy rather than micro-managing everything. These are adults, not children. You don't need to babysit them. Try to really understand and know your team. Everyone is motivated by different things. If you have a university student for example, can you work around their study hours and make sure they can balance everything.

For employees with families, probably the most important thing for them is flexibility. If you can work flexibility into their work arrangement that's far more important than a pay raise. And the same with bonuses. Think about what motivates that person. Don't give them a gift voucher unless it's a really special gift. Always try to think about what that person would love. And usually it's not the most expensive thing. It's that care. Get something that shows — *Yes, I understand more about you and you're more than just an employee. You're a real team member and we love having you as part of our team.*

Your business must have a 'flexibility factor'. It brings the best out in people if you can adapt to their life. For example, mothers coming back to work, can you provide school-friendly hours, or part time hours? Look at ways to combine lifestyle and work. You get far better results from people when they can work around what works for them too.

ENCOURAGE PERSONAL GROWTH *AND* OFFER CAREER GROWTH

Growing a business and growing your employees go hand-in-hand. The best way to have engaged team members is to provide them with new growth opportunities; keep extending them. Allow them to make mistakes and grow.

If there aren't any external opportunities like conferences and training, look at some internal shifts within the company. Can they take on more responsibility in an area they enjoy? Or is there a fresh skill they are personally interested in? Now it might be a little shift, for example, they may have some writing skills and enjoy writing outside of the office. Perhaps they want to write or edit your newsletter.

Most people want to keep learning and improving their skills so they can advance in their careers and feel a sense of growth. Support and encourage them through new training programs, mentoring and even tuition for work-related courses.

Have a day where everyone writes down their dream career goals and see if your workplace can provide these opportunities.

If your team feel like they're stuck in the same mundane job for the rest of their lives, they'll quickly lose motivation. Promoting team members from within shows that you're committed to helping your team grow and learn. This doesn't mean that you stop bringing in people from outside the team to fill open positions, but regularly promoting your employees will build trust and increase morale.

I'm not a believer in the old system of being promoted and rewarded according to the length of time you have worked somewhere. It shouldn't matter what age people are. Some people want to work their way up the career ranks whereas others don't. Naturally, it's important not to overlook your most loyal staff members, nor do you want to embarrass them. This is why communication is vital — you want to know who wants more responsibility and who doesn't. Who can handle a new dynamic role and who can't. Often you may get someone with a different skillset that is perfect to grow your business — use it. Empower the team to recognise that and discuss it. Explain that the team has many different people with different passions, interests and motivations.

Be open to letting them know you are open to finding the best ways to use their special skills.

EMPOWER YOUR TEAM TO BE DECISION MAKERS AND FUNMAKERS

Team empowerment will do more for your business than you can do if you clone yourself. Empower them to make decisions for your business and provide the wow factor to your clients. Give them permission to go the extra mile. Remind them that they're in the "fun business" and impressing clients is the game.

If your business has got a strong vision, they will understand what you're wanting to achieve. So you can encourage team members to make decisions in line with the vision — their decisions will be positive. So when they do anything, they can ask themselves, 'Is that the vision of the business?' 'Should I do this? Is that part of the vision?' This shows the way through action.

Empower your team to provide extra-awesome customer service. One of our restaurants used to offer to walk people to their car. Many young women felt uncomfortable walking to a car park alone at night, we would ensure that a staff member or two would walk with them, or if it was raining, hold an umbrella over them. It's not an expensive thing to do, it's just that some people don't focus on the small things that make the biggest difference.

You get extra brownie points for doing just those little things. Sure, it can be easy to give away a free drink, but I don't think people remember that as much as some sort of extra service or extra caring factor. As Walt Disney said, "Just do your best work — then try to trump it."

International Mexican restaurant Taco Bell are in the delight business. Back in 2012, a elaborate hoax went around the small Alaskan community of Bethel saying that a Taco Bell restaurant was coming to town. Though it was a joke driven by juveniles, the tiny town of only 6000 people got excited. The closest Taco Bell was 4 hours away and they thought one would now be on their doorstep.

Once word got out that it was a prank, and people were upset and disappointed — Taco Bell jumped into action. They airlifted a Taco Bell truck to the town filled with 10,000 tacos.

Now, that's going the extra mile. But of course, very few have the marketing budget to airlift a massive truck to a remote town, right?

But the point is this: it's not how elaborate the gesture, it's the gesture of thought. Remember the Kool Mints story? That cost me less than $5 but it got me a customer for life and a raving and loyal fan. I may not have airlifted a truck, but it built a genuine long-lasting relationship.

If you focus on empowering your team and develop their self-esteem, they will rise to any occasion. Even those who aren't in leadership roles like to have some power and decision-making ability. They want to feel honoured and trusted and given a chance to learn and develop. Now of course, you set guidelines. Guidelines are important. Like, they're got to turn up for work and they can't just take days off without telling you. They can't turn up in shorts and a t-shirt to a formal event. So you've got the basic guidelines, but also your vision and culture. These guidelines act as good supportive rails for your team to feel empowered to act in the best interest of others without checking with you every second.

SEE PROBLEMS AS OPPORTUNITIES

Any business is going to run into problems at some point in time. It's part of the game. But problems are great! Because when you run into them (which you will) it helps you rectify the system, improve strategies or find new opportunities to deal with them.

And I used to always say to my team, "Don't come to me with problems, come to me with an idea or two towards solving the problem."

Yes, I want to know about the problem but it's important to encourage solutions rather than running full-pelt at the boss or a senior member with a problem.

Now I don't care if they can't find a solution or if ideas are wrong, but actively searching for solutions is a fantastic life skill and if you don't work it, it won't grow. But if you try, it can be amazing what you might be able to come up with. If you're involved in seeing the problem and the consequences, then maybe you have a better understanding than anyone else does. Putting time into resolutions is more beneficial to a business than constantly focusing on the problems.

If someone in the team makes a mistake, empower them to rectify it and ask where they need help. Encourage them not to be embarrassed. Show them that mistakes are really important opportunities in growing the business system and creating raving fans.

Sometimes, I used to love it when something went wrong. We would share it with team members and look for ways to turn that failure into a wow factor? If one of our restaurants had a couple arrive that looked grumpy (maybe they fought in the car or had a particularly bad day) — we would work extra hard to turn that around. We would remind ourselves we're in the fun business. People are coming here to have a good time. They're not coming to have a lousy time. They're not coming here just to eat. They're coming here to enjoy themselves. How can we brighten their day? How can we give them smiles?

If someone left a bad review for example, we would all gather around and find solutions. We would rectify things as a team. Sometimes I would call them up personally and chat to them. It wasn't about offering free dinners or drinks, we never did that, it was about listening and caring and asking for the opportunity to rectify the situation.

Problems only stay as problems if you don't actively search for and encourage solutions.

CELEBRATE GOALS AND ACHIEVEMENTS

Do you celebrate your wins? Or do you just move onto the next goal?

Taking time to praise, acknowledge and appreciate a job done right, speaks volumes. Everybody likes to be appreciated and there's no better way to do it than to acknowledge people in front of their peers or managers.

Celebrate your 'small wins' and the big milestones. A team that feels a sense of achievement feels valued and recognised. Maybe offer a gift or some time off for a job well done.

Behavioural scientist, from the Harvard Business School, Dr Ashley Whillans is a specialist on workplace behaviour and motivation. She says,

"Cash matters in people's lives, but it's not all that matters. What really matters in the workplace is helping employees feel appreciated."

Whillans continues to say: "In a lot of organizations, there are no recognition programs for employees whatsoever, so employers need to catch up."[54]

And she is right. Companies with solid employee recognition programs have increased productivity, lower job turnover, and better returns on investment than other companies in the same industries. Recognising employee engagement and work, celebrating team wins and offering rewards and recognition programs are all wonderful ways to keep your team involved and feeling a sense of connectedness.

The Boston Consulting Group conducted an online global study of 200,000 employees from 189 countries in 2014[55], what they found was that "Globally, the most important single job element for all people is appreciation for their work." One Cicero research group investigated what organisations could do to cause employees to produce great work on a consistent basis. Interestingly, recognition was the most necessary factor.

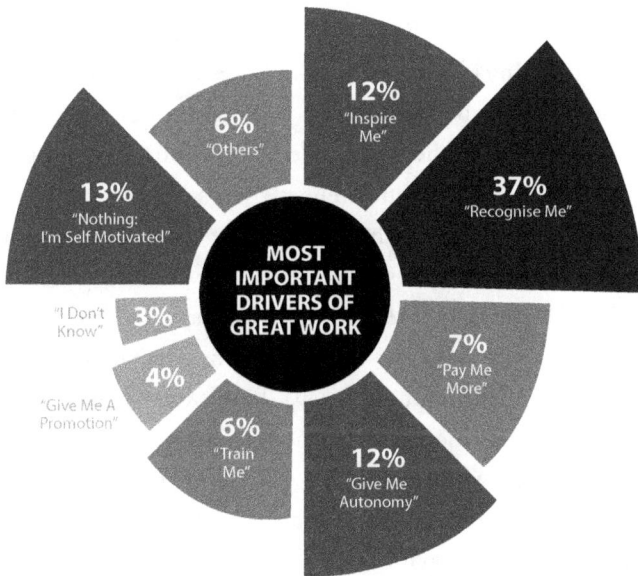

12% "Inspire Me"
6% "Others"
13% "Nothing: I'm Self Motivated"
37% "Recognise Me"
MOST IMPORTANT DRIVERS OF GREAT WORK
"I Don't Know" 3%
"Give Me A Promotion" 4%
7% "Pay Me More"
6% "Train Me"
12% "Give Me Autonomy"

Source: Cicero 2015 research: Employee performance: What causes great work?[56]

Download your 'Employee Morale Booster' worksheet at **deanpublishing.com/smallsurprises**

TEACH THEM THAT UPSELLING IS A DIRTY WORD, BUT S.EX ISN'T

As part of our training, we used to teach upselling. Now, 'upselling' is really important in any business but it's a horrible term to use. It makes people feel uncomfortable and salesy. I don't use that term, but I do explain to our team how small things can make a difference.

I would remind them that these people have come out to have a good time, they're at an expensive restaurant, so they haven't come here to save money. They've come here to have a good night. So, how can we can make the night even better for them? Would they like a well-made cocktail or our French desert? And it's a matter of suggesting, not a hard sell. It's making sure that you offer that second drink or new dessert. How many times have you wanted something else and the waiter was never catching your eye or walking near your table? It's those simple things — like being available and making genuine suggestions.

Make a game with the team. We often made 'upselling' into a fun team game. We'd pick a menu item, perhaps a port or a Pedro Ximenez and we would say, "Okay, who can sell the most of that tonight?" One of my team members was selling bottles of it. Not glasses. The night we had that competition, she sold three bottles of Pedro.

Every week we would do different things like that. Fun stuff, just upselling, but we loved it. It wasn't hard. Our guests loved it. They were coming up to me and saying, "Wow, we've never had some of those foods. That was fantastic. We'd never tried that drink before. What a wonderful drink." So it was a wow experience for them too. But it came from us having a game and having some fun as a team. Our customers enjoyed it and it wasn't a hard sell, we were just having some light-hearted fun. Not one client complained about it. No one said,

"Oh I wasted my money on Pedro."

You must establish fun selling into the culture. It's about, how can we give them a better time? What else can we give them?

Another thing I've noticed is the number of times I don't get a choice to add a tip. People hand you the machine, (because just about everybody pays by credit card nowadays) but there's not even an opportunity to add a tip. You just touch or tap. There's no chance and no discussion to even give a tip even though the machines allow a tip to be added.

We always trained our team when they offered the bill, to say, "If you've had a great time, now is the chance if you would like to tip." And it was "if you'd like to" — it was never a hard sell. It was an opportunity, and if some didn't tip, that was fine, we didn't make them feel bad. Others were very generous. But, the point is: if you don't provide that opportunity, how can people do it?

Even though we don't have a tipping culture in Australia, like America, where you've got to tip 20%, and they push for it and tell you. In Australia, our culture means that tipping is a lovely gesture. And there still are people who do that, especially travellers. Overseas travellers are used to tipping. But if you don't give people the opportunity, that can hurt your team.

So we used to role play that 'paying the bill' moment and make it feel comfortable. We would role play offering suggestions. Like what else could you say to people? What else could you do? And if people have raved about and told you how good you are and what a lovely time they've had, the chances are they'd want to tip. At least allow them the opportunity without embarrassing them.

If you're not the tipping type, here's a little story that may help you see the gesture in a different way:

In the 'old days' when an ice cream sundae cost much less, a 10-year-old boy with ginger hair entered a small cafe and sat at a table. A waitress came over.

"How much is an ice cream sundae?" he asked.

"50 cents," replied the waitress.

The little boy pulled his hand out of his pocket and fossicked with the small number of coins he held.

"How much is a dish of plain ice cream?" he enquired.

Some people were now waiting for a table and the waitress was growing impatient.

"35 cents," she said smiling.

The little boy again counted the coins. "I'll have the plain ice cream, please" he said.

The waitress brought the ice cream, put the bill on the table and walked away. The boy finished the ice cream, paid the cashier and left.

When the waitress came back, she began wiping down the table, tears sprung to her eyes when she saw what he had done. Placed neatly beside the empty dish, was 15 cents — her tip.

Even small tips mean a lot.

It's all about language. People aren't sheep, you're not there to coerce them into corners, or use sneaky tricks. It's not a pleasant culture if you evoke an aura of, "You've got to buy from me", and use these subtle little tricks. It's not authentic.

You want to make a sustainable business and you need to make money to do that. So you need to increase the average dollar sale. You need to grow your business and there's some easy ways to do that without coercion or force.

FIVE EASY WAYS TO CONVERT SALES

1. **More prospects:** Start with your prospects.
2. **Percentage:** Look at what percentages of prospects you convert to customers or clients.

3. **Increase in dollar spend:** Assess how often you increase your average dollar spend with those customers.
4. **Frequency:** Then look at how often they come back. So frequency of purchase.
5. **Margin:** Ensure there is an adequate financial margin between what you sell and the price that you sell it for.

These five principles make a huge difference in growing your business. Most business owners understand the principles, but when you actually develop them through providing a better service, it truly increases sales. Or as I prefer to call it the S. EX — The Surprise Experience.

Use the delightful Surprise EXperience! Over and over again. No matter what business you think you're in, you're in the fun business. You've come to give people a great time. You've come to delight and deliver.

Offer suggestions to make their experience special. Ask your team: How can we give them a better time? What else can we give them? How can we make them smile? For restaurants, offer a cocktail when they arrive. People don't always have cocktails, so it's special.

And yes, the rules say it is 'upselling' but make it fun. It's really about the customers' experience. How can you improve that for them? Give them opportunities to enjoy their time more. It's a whole mindset shift.

And with your team, engage with them and ask them "How we can convert people into raving fans?" They get engaged and excited about it too. But if you say, "Okay, today we're upselling", they all shut off. They hate it. They don't want to feel uncomfortable. So come from another angle and explain that it's all about the customer. And yes, it grows our business and it makes us much better at what we do. Them makes us stand out from our competitors. You don't have to say, "This makes us more money." Say, "Yeah it makes us more sustainable. We can grow and develop. But it's about the customer. It's giving them an exceptional experience." Because that energy is authentic and doesn't make people feel money-orientated.

That's why I like talking about Delight and how can you delight people. Read more about sales in Part 3.

Download your free worksheet '5 Ways Calculator: Prospects to Profit' at **deanpublishing.com/ smallsurprises**

HOW PERSONALITY AND LEADERSHIP STYLES INFLUENCE THE WAY YOU WORK

WHO ARE YOU *REALLY* TALKING TO?

Each year, thousands of companies around the world use the DISC tool to determine their employees' common behavioural styles and patterns. These are classified as:

D — Dominance
I — Influence
S — Steadiness
C — Conscientiousness

And/or the combination of all four.

When I first began training as a DISC coach with Assessments 24x7 (assessments24x7.com) and using these tools, it changed the way I did business. It gave me an insight into people and what made them really tick. It also allowed me to address people in a communication style that *they* understood. It helped me become a better leader and listener.

We began to dissolve any team conflicts within minutes and discovered new ways to work with all different personality types. Essentially, it's a tool that works for everyone. There is no down-side to understanding people better and talking their language.

D STYLES

D

DOMINANCE
DETERMINED
DEMANDING
DRIVEN
DOERS

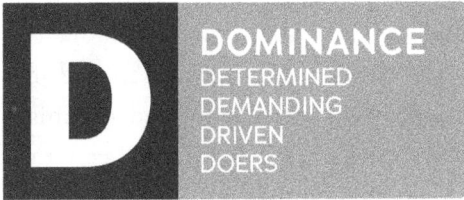

D-styles are classified as dominant people. They're the leaders. They're the people who want results. They're very results-driven. They often get bored with detail and avoid details (unless it gets results). So when you're dealing with those sort of people, you need to let them make the decision, because they are natural decision-makers.

Allow them to lead and make the final decision, otherwise you'll lose them. They are often assertive and they love making things happen. They're competitive and like to win.

D's are often team leaders, CEOs or firm owners. Because D's are competitive, they want to be in charge, they thrive in high-ranking positions.

Typical D-style occupations: leaders, CEOs, Presidents.
Strengths: Great decision-makers, competitive, assertive, leader.
Weaknesses: Can be intolerant with a slower pace or indecisiveness.

I STYLES

I

INFLUENCE
IMPRESSIVE
INTERACTIVE
INSPIRING
INITIATORS

I's are the influencers. They are generally enthusiastic and love people. But they want to be liked. So, in dealing with them, you must spend time with them and find out what interests them, because it's really important to them that you like them. They will like you, they like everybody. They really want to like people, which can sometimes get them into trouble because they trust easily.

High I's love to name drop and let you know who they know. Not because they're arrogant, but because they are great networkers and they thrive in being involved with people. They're friendly and optimistic which in many ways makes them easier to sell to, if you gain their confidence and you praise them. Make them feel great.

Whereas praising a D wouldn't work. They're results driven, they want tasks, not people. I's are far more interested in people and want to spend time with people and talk to them, rather than getting on with the job. And that can be frustrating too, because often they don't complete tasks. I's are more worried about getting on well with people, they miss the point sometimes. They're not looking at the detail. They're more interested in how they're getting on with people.

Typical I-style occupations: sales, TV personalities, hosts, entertainers.
Strengths: communication, friendly, optimistic, influential, networker, inspiring.
Weaknesses: can be overly talkative, gets distracted, trusts too easily.

S STYLES

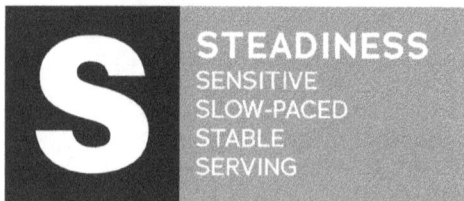

STEADINESS
SENSITIVE
SLOW-PACED
STABLE
SERVING

S-styles stand for the steadiness factor. These people are sincere, sensitive, patient and very modest. They really care about other people. They hate change. You've got to be so careful with them. So, anything you want to change, you have to lead them to it gradually, because it's outside their comfort zone. But they're great people in a team because they care about the others in the team. They make sure the other team members are being looked after, doing their jobs, giving them confidence. So it's a really important team member, a real motherly sort of influence in a team.

Typical S-style occupations: Human Resources manager, therapist, counsellor, executive assistant, customer service manager.

Strengths: sincere, patient, concerned for others, team players.

Weaknesses: resistant to change, too concerned about others, needs to be more assertive.

C STYLES

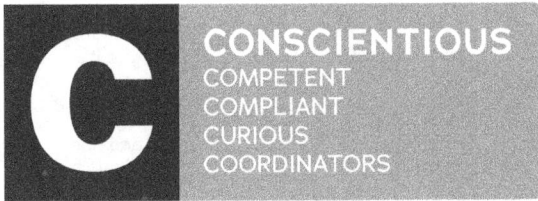

C's are compliance people. They're definitely task-orientated. They want things to be finished. They're accurate. They have a real attention to detail. They're very cautious because they take a long time to make a decision, because they've got to get all the information together and assess everything. They can also take forever to make a decision because they still want to get more and more information, to make sure they're making the right decision. They're better off combined with a D-style person, who wants to get on and is results driven, whereas the C's keep wanting more information. They're contemplative people, they're very cautious. But it's a great trait to have in a business where you've got to have an attention to detail, when you've got to make sure things are correct and accurate. So that's a great skill to have in your team.

Typical C-style occupations: researchers, scientists, editors.

Strengths: attention to detail, accuracy, informative, curious, cooperative.

Weaknesses: can be slow decision makers, driven to get more and more information.

	D	I	S	C
VOICE (Match yours to theirs)	Rapid pace Limited emotion	Rapid pace Friendly, upbeat	Slow pace Warm and caring	Moderate pace Formal, businesslike
COMMUNICATION DO'S (Approaches that cause them to 'open up')	Focus on results Be brief and to the point Exhibit confidence Expect them to be blunt Don't overreact to it	Expect them to be talkative and stray off the topic – don't let them take you off track Make them the centre of attention	Break the ice first Expect them to be slow, methodical and calm Give them 'time to think' Listen attentively	Expect them to want a lot of information, and be prepared to give it Repond logically and not emotionally
COMMUNICATION DONT'S (Approaches that cause them to 'shut down')	Don't ramble Avoid 'chit chat' Don't challenge them, you will lose Don't offer assurance you cannot deliver	Don't be cold or rude Don't be too businesslike Don't talk down to them Avoid dwelling on the fine print or details	Don't force a quick response Don't interrupt them Don't mistake their willingness to 'go along' as agreement	Avoid being too personal or informal Don't get too close to them and no touching
MOVEMENT STYLE	Fast and direct movements They know where they are going Focused	Can be the 'social butterfly', ensuring to say "hello" to everyone before beginning a task	Slow movements, steady and not quick to rush things	Moderate and more formal in their movements, not a touchy-feely person

THE BEAUTY IN THE DISC TEAM COMBINATION

Like many great teams, the power is in the diversity. The combination of these styles really provides a foundation for success.

You've got your D-style dominant person, who's actually running the show and making sure you achieve results and remaining competitive in the industry. You've got your I-styles to make sure that everyone's happy and getting on well together, often they're also the sales people. You've got the C-styles keeping the accuracy and detail on track to make sure there are no mistakes or small details missing. Then you have the S-style people giving the steadiness to the company and team, making sure the team are well looked after.

Understanding these styles really helps build a high-performance team that not only performs well but communicate effectively.

REMINDER: In dealing with each of these four main personalities, bear in mind everyone's got a bit of each style within them — and it's not all one style, but there will be a stronger dominant style that fits your personality.

IT'S ALL ABOUT COMMUNICATION

Learning these styles is all about using the most effective person for each role and understanding how to communicate with each style.

If you have someone in the team that loves talking to people, that cares about other people, empower them to be in the service sector of the business. Empower them to use their natural skillset. If you have someone that loves to make decisions and move projects forward — utilise that skill.

NATURAL STYLES AND ADAPTED STYLES

The DISC profile tool helps us see our *Natural Style* and our *Adapted Style*.

Our Natural Style is as the name suggests — it's what comes naturally to you. It's how you naturally perceive, interpret, and interact with the world and others. Some people are naturally more task-orientated whereas others prefer people.

How we operate, respond or learn to behave within our environment is our Adapted Style. Naturally your work and home environments may bring out different styles, and you can have two different styles of behaviours in different environments, though our Natural Style is consistent, the Adapted Style depends on the environment and the task that needs to be done.

The more you steer away from your Natural Style to adapt, the greater stress you tend to feel.

When you're working in an environment where you have to change or suppress your natural way of being — or where your natural skills aren't used or appreciated — the greater potential for stress, work conflicts and performance problems.

Now of course, a certain amount of adaptation is necessary for any work environment, you're not going to turn up in trackpants and Ugg boots and say that "naturally you like to dress comfortably" — you're going to adapt to the work situation and dress professionally. Adaption is important and necessary — but when adapted crushes your natural tendencies in the way that you behave and relate to people — it can clash!

When the Natural Style is similar to your Adapted Style, you're far more comfortable and it's less stressful. If you can behave in the work place in your Natural Style, then there's not much conflict.

For example, if you're a C-style and you're trying to sell, it could get stressful because you're more about detail and you're naturally task-orientated, but to sell you've got to be people-orientated, and that's going to be stressful. It's not saying that you can't or shouldn't do it, anyone can learn new skills, but it's probably going to be more stressful at the beginning because it's not natural to you.

Being aware of your style helps you cope with stress. If you realise that you've got a weakness in a certain area, once you're aware of that and you're prepared to work on it and improve it, you can change it. That's where the adaption will come through. And, after a while, it will probably improve your natural style too.

Because we act and behave different in different environments, if you change jobs or have new expectations within your current job (such as moving more into management) that will take a different skillset to what you're used to. So you will need to develop other skills and that will affect your Natural Style and also your Adapted Style.

It boils down to being smart — to understanding people's styles. The round pegs in round holes scenario. When you can see that somebody is feeling uncomfortable, it's usually not their natural place. It may not be that they're not good at their role, it may be that the role is not natural for them and they need to be placed in a position that allows them to shine or they need more time and education to adapt.

REMINDERS

Recently, one of my clients from a real estate firm used the DISC profile for their team. After discovering each other's styles they decided to use abbreviations over their desks to remind them how to treat the other individuals within the team. They made a huge effort to treat the individual how they wanted to be treated. The signs created a bit of banter, which also helped improve the culture.

Here's some example of signs you can make for the office or workplace.

> *Hi, I am Jane.*
> *I'm a **D-style** so I love taking quick action and getting results! If you need me to make a decision — then I'm ready and raring to go. Bring it on!*
>
> *P.S: Sometimes I'm a little too results-driven and forget to be diplomatic. Oops. Don't take it personally, I just get so focused that I sometimes overlook other details.*

Hi, I'm Jenny,

I'm an **I-style** — which means I love people and enjoy knowing about you. I'm dynamic, friendly and approachable.

PS: If I get a little chatty and off topic, please gently (kindly) nudge me back to task. I often care so much about people that I miss the detail.

Hi, I am Gary.

I'm a **S-style**. I love a stable and warm environment, it brings out my best. I am a great team player and a natural listener. If you need a collaborative person on your project — then I'm your guy!

P.S: Just be aware I'm not keen on spontaneous unscripted change or making decisions if I don't have all the necessary details. I love the details.

Hi, I'm Steven,

I am a **C-style**. I enjoy focusing on tasks and attention to detail. If you need someone to dot your i's and cross your t's - then look no further.

PS- I like to have all the facts and data before I make a decision. I am a logical thinker, so please give me plenty of time to weigh up all the details first.

LEARNING STYLES

It's also important to look into people's individual learning style. Are they more auditory or visual? What's their preferred style? That way you can adjust your coaching style to match their learning style. Or your management style for your team.

The VAK Learning Styles Model[57] was developed way back in the 1920s and used extensively by psychologists to classify the most common ways in which people learn. They realised that many people prefer to learn in one of three ways: visual, auditory or kinaesthetic. Although, they also knew that most of us blend these three styles.

- **Visual:** a visually-dominant learner absorbs and retains information better when it is presented in picture form, diagrams, photos or charts.
- **Auditory:** an auditory-dominant learner prefers listening. They often respond best to sounds, such as voices in a lecture or group discussion. They often use audiobooks or music.
- **Kinaesthetic:** a kinaesthetic-dominant learner prefers a physical experience. They like applied learning and thrive in a "hands-on" environment. They respond well to being able to touch or feel an object or learning prop.

In more recent times, this learning model has developed further and a number of new learning systems have evolved incorporating some additional styles like reading, writing and combinations of styles together. All in all, the idea is to highlight people's more natural and preferred method of learning, remembering and organising things best in their minds.

ENGAGE A VISUAL LEARNER

"I like to see information, then speak."

- Give them well presented slides with colour and diagrams
- Use whiteboards, Smartboards, PowerPoint presentations
- Give well-presented handouts with photos/diagrams/charts
- Give them study guides or textbooks to keep

ENGAGE AN AUDITORY LEARNER

"I like to hear information, then speak."

- Allow them to hear speakers or lecturers on subjects they're interested in
- Use audiobooks or guided online learning programs
- Embed videos that they can hear (not only watch)
- They thrive hearing stories or participating vocally in groups
- Make recordings
- Get them to read out loud

ENGAGE A KINAESTHETIC LEARNER

"I love to move and use my body to learn."

- Use 'hands on' learning methods or get them to move while learning
- Do role playing
- Conduct learning experiments
- Use activities or team bonding sessions to engage them
- On-the-job training is great for them[58]

ENGAGE A READING/WRITING LEARNING STYLE

"I like to read and take notes to learn best."

- Ask them to review what they have learned
- Journal writing or taking notes of the meetings
- Use books that they are interested in
- Ask them to write the team newsletter
- Use words
- They would rather read by themselves than have someone read to them to intake information

Want to know your DISC style? Contact me for a comprehensive assessment.

Want to know your DISC style? Contact me for a comprehensive assessment at **deanpublishing. com/smallsurprises**

PART THREE

SALES FOUNDATIONS AND EQ

"Great salespeople are relationship builders who provide value and help their customers win."

Jeffrey Gitomer

PUTTING SOME STYLE
BACK INTO SALES

Here's something not everyone knows: *Everyone is in SALES.*
Yes, even if you class yourself as a receptionist or the concierge – you're in sales. If you're the local plumber – you're in sales. If you're the CEO of a massive finance company – yep, you're in sales too.

Most people will buy from people they trust. If they like you, they'll listen to you, and that lets you be able to establish a rapport, but they won't buy from you until they trust you. Bottom line. Sure, minor sales like a loaf of bread may not come into the equation – but if you're trying to sell a larger product or service, then you can bet your bottom dollar – that trust really matters.

So, anyone who is in business, if you're dealing with people — **you're in sales.**

Even if you're not dealing directly with people – like a vet, sure, who've got to make sure that the animals are treated well, but you also have to explain things about each animal to its owners. If the owners don't trust you, why would they allow their beloved pet to be treated by you.

You are always representing that company or brand regardless of the title you hold. People are making decisions based on how they are treated and the level of trust they feel. This happens at all levels of business – not just the top. In fact, most of the public never meet the woman or man that owns the company. They meet someone who works for the company.

SLEEZY SALES VERSUS REAL SALES

Most people squirm when they hear the word 'sales'. They think of the hideous sleezy salespeople that try to manipulate, coerce or force people to buy. And we all know how much we detest those types! You know the type, the one that holds you hostage and requires a direct and firm "no way" to get the point.

No one likes overly pushy salespeople. But good salespeople aren't like that. They are caring, listening types that love to provide great services.

When I talk to a new team about their sales strategies, I always ask them how they feel about sales. I ask them to write down what they genuinely believe about sales. And often I read all kinds of negative things like, pushy, cheesy, forceful. This is the stereotype we often see and dread.

But I talk to them about helping people. What about providing a service? What about solving a problem? What about making people feel good about their purchase? What about showing how much easier it's going to be and how you or your product solves their problem?

To me, that is *real sales*.

I often remind people that if you believe in your product or service, wouldn't that mean you want the best for others? That you would like to help them and know what's important to them? How you can provide that solution for them? Wouldn't you or your company be the best for them? Or would you prefer that they went to your competitors that offer a second-grade service?

So, if you work from that angle, you can help the team realise that they are helping people. You're not just trying to sell a product, you're giving people something better. Change the whole way you think about sales. So, that it's about providing a product or a service that the client needs to solve a problem that they've got. Simple.

It's about building trust, it's about providing solutions, it's not about how to sell it, it's not about the money. If you're proud of your product and you know it's good, you don't need to do a hard sell.

Be proud of building relationships. If you build the relationship, they'll come back time and again. That's how you disrupt things too – people come to you and then they refer their friends and associates. And that referral is far better than any sale because somebody else told them how good you are, how good your product is. That's what selling really should be. That's what clever salespeople do. They don't just flog products or push too hard. They build genuine relationships and offer solutions.

They build a brand the people can trust and want to be a part of.

4 SALES STYLES YOU NEED TO AVOID

THE ORDER-TAKER

Order-takers just literally take orders. They take your order and then they don't try to do anything else. They don't ask any questions, they simply just do the very basics.

That's cool, if someone wants to buy a sandwich quickly. But there's so much more they could be doing, introducing other items, building a good relationship so customers will return. Order takers just do the order. They take a sale and do the minimum paperwork. They haven't discussed anything else or offered any other benefits. They are coasters. Just coasting along not offering anything special.

THE OVERSELLER

They promise the world and deliver less. That is the worst thing to do because you need to be over-delivering rather than over-selling. The overseller often just loves making the sale as an adrenaline rush not as a genuine service.

They can also be known as **The-Sell-Anything-to-Anyone-at-Anytime Type**. They promise everything and often get shocked as to why people feel let down when 'they gave them such a good deal'. They often love money and status. Sales is their passion but they've got to learn emotional intelligence.

THE PRODUCT PUSHERS

Product pushers are pushy and annoying. They talk about the product and want to push it regardless of whether it's a right fit for the customer or not. They think in terms of short-term sales or KPIs rather than long-term customer satisfaction. Sure, they are happy to door-knock or cold call but they often fail to listen to the customers objections and take their 'no thank you' seriously.

They'll be the type that keeps calling you even if you've said 'no' three times to their face. They care about how many items they sell, not the people they sell to.

THE OVER-STATER

Then you've got the salespeople who don't listen to their clients because they just love hearing their own voice. They love over-stating why you should buy from them. They love spruiking about who uses their product or service.

They don't listen to the person, they tell people about themselves. It's all about them, their product, how good they are, or how good their services are. But they're not listening to what the client needs. They are over-stating their value and under-stating the customers' value. They often name drop and assume you're interested in status.

THE BEST SALESPERSON IS THE SOLUTION SOLVER

The best salespeople I have worked with, and the type I love, is the solution solver, or the problem solver. They listen to the client, build genuine trusting relationships and try to help them solve a problem or find a solution. That's how good selling works.

For example, if people are looking for a product to do with a particular job, the solution solver asks, "What do you need?"

They consider: *What's the best way to help them get their needs met?* They are curious and open to investigating solutions for others.

For example, if you're a lawyer, dig down to find out what's important to your client. What are the issues that matter to them most? What are they trying to achieve? Rather than shooting off how good you are as a lawyer or how you can do this and do that, find out what the client wants and then provide what *they* want, not what you want for them.

Yes guide, use your expertise, but listen, empathise and understand first.

The great business mogul Stephen Covey advocates a similar approach when he suggests to his readers: "Seek first to understand, then to be understood."

This is the key. And it's often done through the power of suggestion. Ask your potential client lots of good questions. And yes, you do guide them if you're smart, you're guiding those customers and clients towards a viable solution that will suit them.

The best salespeople build relationships and offer great solutions.

Stay honest and authentic, use supporting documentation if that helps build trust. Don't be down people's throats, I see so many sales people do that. They're flogging their own product and telling you how fabulous it is, but if that doesn't help solve the customers problem – it's irrelevant.

TOUCHPOINTS

Don't be afraid to spend time talking to people. It's simple really. Apple say that there's at least seven touch points before people will buy.[59] And those touch points may be an advertisement they see or a social media post. It might be friends talking about their new computer or iPhone. But some people need lots of touch points before they actually buy a product.

And the same goes for buying a service too. You don't just attack someone, trying to sell your product on the first meeting. You may need to give them more information and build rapport. Sometimes it takes time. Don't go for the jugular on the first call. You need to spend time to build that relationship. So it might be a telephone call, you might follow up with information, you may send other testimonials. All these things build rapport before you ask for the sale.

Sales Surprise – Download this sales chapter for free and give it to your team. Go to **deanpublishing.com/ smallsurprises**

PEOPLE BUY ON EMOTION

When people do buy often it's emotion that is driving their decisions.

Harvard professor Gerald Zaltman, wrote an entire book on this subject titled, *How Customers Think: Essential Insights into the Mind of the Market*[60]. Zaltman suggests that 95 percent of our buying decisions takes place in the subconscious mind.

Despite the fact so many of us *think* that we are making purchasing decisions with our logic and analytical mind, Zaltman's research suggests this isn't the case. He reveals how we are largely driven by unconscious urges, the biggest of which is emotion. Further research shows that our unconscious "decisions" are then often communicated to our conscious mind in a way that makes the conscious mind feel it made the "logical" decision.

For example, you may unconsciously buy something with an inner urge to appear more affluent that you are, and your conscious mind may say *if I buy this I will attract higher paying clients to my business*. Though you feel it was logic making the final decision, the deeper decision was an unconscious emotional one.

Now, you don't have to have a degree in psychology to understand this. You just need to know that buying is very often an emotional choice! Know that one thing and you're already miles ahead of the swarm that still insists to 'push the hard sell'.

You need to understand that what drives people to buy isn't always what you think. Let's take a deeper look.

If you're selling a computer program for example, don't only focus on how easy it is to use and all its bells and whistles – focus on what it may do on a deeper emotional level. Will it make the company look more innovative and professional? Will it make the purchaser look smart in the eyes of his or her boss?

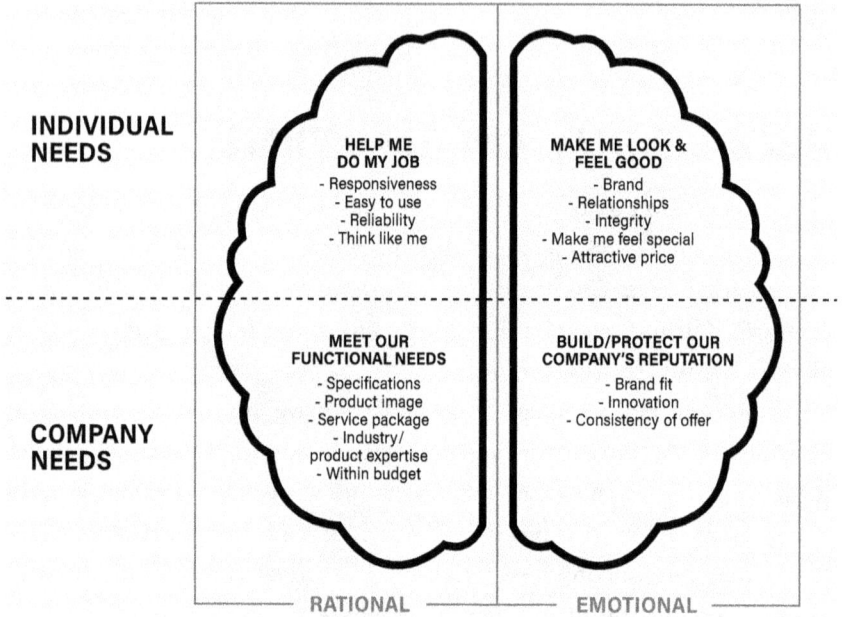

INDIVIDUAL NEEDS

HELP ME DO MY JOB
- Responsiveness
- Easy to use
- Reliability
- Think like me

MAKE ME LOOK & FEEL GOOD
- Brand
- Relationships
- Integrity
- Make me feel special
- Attractive price

MEET OUR FUNCTIONAL NEEDS
- Specifications
- Product image
- Service package
- Industry/product expertise
- Within budget

BUILD/PROTECT OUR COMPANY'S REPUTATION
- Brand fit
- Innovation
- Consistency of offer

COMPANY NEEDS

RATIONAL — EMOTIONAL

Get a copy of this image for your sales team to pin it up in the office. Go to **deanpublishing.com/smallsurprises** to get a free copy today!

Obviously don't just bark these options out and hope that they hit the emotional point of the customer. You need to listen and stay attuned to their deeper needs. Listen and observe, seek to understand what drives them. Does it help them look better, feel better, appear better?

BUYING DECISIONS

RATIONAL

- PRICE
- QUALITY
- FEATURE
- RELIABILITY
- WARRANTY

EMOTIONAL

- LOOK
- FEEL
- ESTEEM
- BRAND
- SAFETY
- FEAR

EMOTION CREATES THE BUYING MOTION

"People don't buy for logical reasons. They buy for emotional reasons."

— *Zig Ziglar*

It's important to educate yourself on emotional buying. To see it as a skill not a flaw or a process in which to manipulate people. Understand that buying is largely built on emotion and your sales will flourish.

THREE KEY POINTS

1. Understand that buying is (very) often an emotional choice.
2. Know your *emotional* unique selling points or niche. Script them if possible.
3. Delight your clients!

You must look for ways to DELIVER and DELIGHT – create your own niche that's based around emotion.

Teach your sales team how to make a sale, it's not all about 'sex on the first date' — it doesn't always work, it repels people. You need to woo people. You need to spend the time to create a relationship. You need to understand their buying decisions.

Great businesses teach their sales team how to understand the buying needs of their clients and how to build genuine relationships with potential and existing customers.

Be patient. Be patient to realise that it's more important to build that relationship, so people feel more comfortable to buy, and more importantly, to stay around and buy again. The best customers and clients keep coming back for more because you truly care for them and want to address their needs. They also become your greatest advocates, they really trust you and feel as though they've been treated special with individualised customer service. Because they have. And they'll love to tell their friends all about you.

Whereas a salesperson who just goes in and spends all their time talking about the product and just trying too hard, repels people. It's not even appealing to their emotion or reason for buying.

Now some people say, "That's great Milton, but KPI's are critical, I need my sales team to sell not love people."

I always tell them, "I love KPI's too but don't create a culture solely around achieving KPIs without training your team on how to achieve those KPI's intelligently and without using long-term customer service that emotionally DELIGHTS your customers."

Train your team to identify the type of client they are dealing with. Identifying them early would probably make a potentially frustrating sale a very seamless and easy process. If your team can see and understand whether they are dealing with a D-style or a C-style — the sale becomes easier for them and buying becomes easier for the customer — because you're meeting them at their level, in their preferred method of decision-making or processing.

Train your team to be mindful of emotion. Make your entire team emotionally intelligent! Put the customer in their comfort zone and listen to them. This helps you assess if they are task-orientated or people-orientated. Are they open or are they closed? How do they prefer to be treated? What emotional needs are they looking for?

If you teach your team to pick up on those inner clues, the entire sales process becomes a hundred times easier and selling becomes seamless.

SELLING TO A D-STYLE

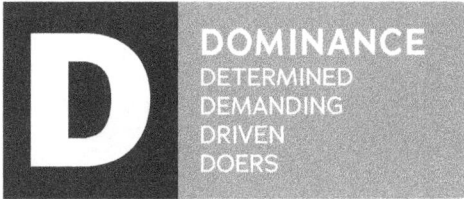

D DOMINANCE
DETERMINED
DEMANDING
DRIVEN
DOERS

When you're making a sale to a dominant person, don't spend too much time on the detail. They must have the information quick. They're going to ask a couple of big questions but they want a quick answer so you must know your stuff. Don't harp on about all the nuances and details of the product unless they ask. They just want to know that it's going to work, and get on with it. Be prepared for them to make a quick buying decision and have the paperwork ready and do it for them if you can. They're busy and don't want to stuff around. They pay and go.

SELLING TO A I-STYLE

I INFLUENCE
IMPRESSIVE
INTERACTIVE
INSPIRING
INITIATORS

Selling to an I is all about them. How they would feel and how it will elevate their status amongst their friends. You can tell them about some celebrities or leaders that have used your product or service. They love to be cared about and asked about, so don't be afraid to ask them lots of questions about them. They'll love you for it.

Really go for the relationship bonding first – they will love the attention and then they'll tell all their friends. They are positive and enthusiastic types – so match their nature and they'll enjoy the process.

SELLING TO A S-STYLE

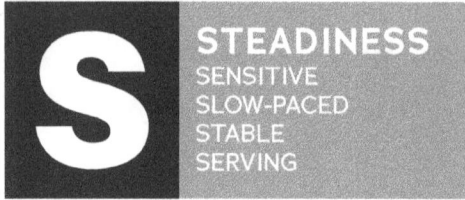

S
STEADINESS
SENSITIVE
SLOW-PACED
STABLE
SERVING

S-style often care more about you than themselves. They're really patient people. They want to make sure everyone's included. So when asking them questions, allow time for slower answers and decisions. Keep the process steady and give them all the detail they ask for. Be sensitive to their needs and listen carefully. Don't push for a quick sale but give them space and time to make their own decision.

SELLING TO A C-STYLE

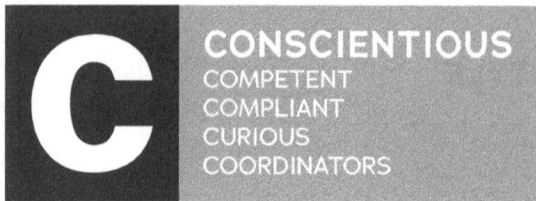

C
CONSCIENTIOUS
COMPETENT
COMPLIANT
CURIOUS
COORDINATORS

It's all about dotting their i's and crossing their t's. They want detail and will often make a slow and well thought out decision. Don't push them to make a decision without all the details because they'll feel really uncomfortable. Give them the inside information and perhaps even some manuals or instructions if you're selling a product. Reassure them that you'll find out any answers to their questions and allow them time to arrive at a decision.

THE TOP 4 *MISTAKES IN SALES*

#1. LACK OF CONSISTENCY

You've got to have a consistent product or service. If you're a service-based company, you've got to turn up on time. Many tradespeople don't turn up on time and that's really frustrating for most people. Or they don't clean up. It's really basic stuff. But because most of us don't know how technically good an electrician is, as long as the lights work, we're happy. But we have no idea what's happening behind the scenes. If they turn up on time, if they care, if they clean up, and they fix the problem, then that is important to us.

#2. NOT LISTENING

I can't emphasise the importance of listening enough. Don't try and be all things for everybody – but make sure you listen to their needs, not yours. Make sure, if you're a niche market that you can provide a service or a product that fulfils their needs. If you can't, move on and recommend elsewhere, or let them know upfront that you can't help them. They'll respect you more for that too, rather than making a bad sale.

#3. DON'T SELL CRAP OR OVER-PROMISE AND UNDER DELIVER

If you don't believe in your product or service, either change it, improve it or get another product. You can't sell crap and feel good about your sales. Period.

A real salesperson is offering help, solutions and solving problems – not creating more.

If you're going to return a phone call, provide extra information, do it! It's always the biggest frustration when someone says that they will do something but fail or forget to do it. But now, with great sales funnels, there's so much great software out there to help your sales process or act as reminders.

#4. NO SALES PROCESS

You need to implement a sales process. Know your steps and processes. Step one is a contact, then you might provide a quote, then you follow it up. Use systems and processes to support your BEFORE and AFTER sales processes. Do you have a process for getting testimonials or asking for an online review? You're building relationships all the time and you need processes you can follow and measure. Follow up, follow up, follow up. If you say that you'll get back to them, then do it. Don't just leave your sales processes in the hands of the gods – be active and attentive. Follow up on every part of the sales process: before, after and during.

⚜ 3 OF THE BEST SALES TOOLS EVER ⚜

1. **DELIGHT** – your clients and potential clients (use emotion, surprise and care)
2. **DISRUPT**– your current industry (do what your competitors aren't)
3. **DELIVER** – always, every time (be consistently great

Repeat!

After you have done that, then ask this one question: *how can we improve on that?*

MEASURE IT

How can you know your sales figures if you're not measuring them? You must measure what matters, and your sales stream matters!

You need to know your conversion rates so you can assess what works and what doesn't.

But remember: just because someone hasn't purchased from you doesn't mean they're not a customer. Maybe they didn't buy from you but loved your attitude. Maybe they regret buying from a competitor and now tell other people to go to you instead.

Measuring your metrics is important for business but it's also important to realise they don't show you who is singing your praises behind the statistics.

Remember the five easy ways to increase your profit in sales. But also measure it.

1. More prospects: Start with your prospects. How many prospects do you have?

2. Percentage: Look at what percentages of prospects you convert to be customers or clients.

3. Increase in dollar spend: Assess how often you increase your average dollar spend with those customers.

4. Frequency: Look at how often you get customers to come back. So frequency of purchase.

5. Margin: Ensure there is adequate financial margin between what you sell and the price that you sell it for.

But what then? After conversions and sales you must keep your customers in your sales funnels and involved in your activities. This doesn't just mean connecting them to your Facebook – this means, keeping the relationship and nurturing it.

LEADERSHIP OF THE FUTURE

EMOTIONAL INTELLIGENCE

Emotional intelligence (often referred to as **EQ or EI**) is the tool of the future. Emotional intelligence, in my opinion, is a requirement for any leader. It helps people better understand and work with others, it helps people connect and perceive other's emotions and inner drives more easily.

Emotional Intelligence is the ability to control, understand and manage your own emotions as well as be sensitive and open to others emotions. In business, it is also related to understanding that each individual learns differently and being able to give the employees the space to learn and grow in an encouraging environment.[61]

It's imperative to understand people's feelings and respond appropriately in a positive and proactive way. Basically, it's a heart-and-mind performance. It empowers relationships and directs unified teamwork.

Using EQ can help bring out the best in people. They become more motivated and feel a sense of belonging and recognition. Not all people are motivated by money, it's a requirement of course, but people stay in a workplace if their needs are being fulfilled and they feel they have a future there.

As business leaders, we must stay on track to make sure that we are always maintaining healthy models within our companies, therefore, creating happy and healthy environments.

EQ = SELF + RELATIONSHIPS + ENVIRONMENT

According to a report in the *Journal of Personality Assessment* by researchers, Caruso, Mayer & Salovey, the four branches of emotional intelligence include a specific skill set and therefore benefited the individual and everyone around them.[62] These branches include:

1. **Identifying emotions** – Being able to identify and express different emotions accurately.

2. **Emotional facilitation of thought** – the ability to use and generate emotions which facilitate and redirect attention to important events and to be able to harness different emotions encouraging different approaches to problem solving.

3. **Understanding emotions** – this is the ability to understand that emotions are complex and require a deeper understanding. It also enables one to recognise the causes of the emotions and relationship connections to the emotions.

4. Managing emotions – this is when one is self-aware of their own emotions, to be able to determine whether their emotions are clear or reaction-based. Managing emotions is also about actively managing negative emotions rather than suppressing them and dealing with them in a healthy manner.[63]

Through understanding these levels of emotional intelligence, one can then understand the benefits of gaining a stronger EI.

LOW EQ VERSUS HIGH EQ

Many people feel misunderstood and unappreciated and some blame others for the problems at work or in other situations. People with lower levels of emotional intelligence are often subject to communication conflicts, emotional outbursts and moodiness. Some people get angry and hostile during conflict and confrontation rather than sitting back and reflecting on what caused the situation and how to handle it with maturity and empathy. Many don't look beyond the immediate fierce emotion, or the emotional reasons that lay behind that.

People with lower emotional intelligence focus on competition and winning all the time. Though, we all like results, and being a D-style personality myself, I like winning too. But, the best way to win is to have everybody involved and working together as a team.

If you have lower emotional intelligence, it's more difficult to understand what others are thinking or feeling. There is a lack of empathy and connection. Often, people with lower emotional intelligence also have long-term quality relationships because they're not as open to communicating and bonding with other people.

Now, on the other hand, people with high emotional intelligence, learn to adapt to other ways and situations. They are more adaptable, weigh up the situation carefully, and treat people how they want to be treated.

People with high levels of emotional intelligence take responsibility and look for solutions to fix problems. They're creative people too. They take situations on-board and take control of performance and productivity.

They're more self-disciplined, so they don't allow excuses and blaming when working together as a team. They look for win-win solutions too.

The traits of our DISC styles can show us the reactions that happen between someone who has low or high EQ in any given moment.

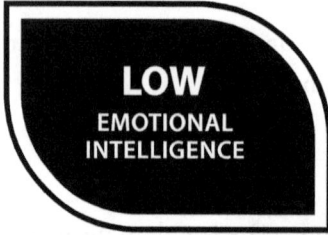

LOW EMOTIONAL INTELLIGENCE		HIGH EMOTIONAL INTELLIGENCE
Aggressive Demanding Ego-Driven Bossy Confrontational	**D** TYPE	Assertive Ambitious Driven Certain Decisive
Easily Distracted Insincere Selfish Self Indulgent Impulsive	**I** TYPE	Social Positive Considerate Charismatic Influential
Resistant to Change Passive Unemotional Slow Stubborn	**S** TYPE	Patient Consistent Stable Precise Structured
Critical Choosy Fussy Hard to Please Perfectionistic	**C** TYPE	Detailed Careful Selective Systematic High Standards

SALES FOUNDATIONS AND EQ

CONSCIOUS AND CARING CEOS OF THE 21ST CENTURY

It has become crucial for business leaders in the 21st century to be highly emotionally intelligent in order to succeed. Having a high EI also allows one to create stronger connections within the business, stronger relationships within teams and staff members and a higher success rate.

Business evolution will also require each individual to take responsibility for their own emotional intelligence. By effectively showing that you, as a business leader have a high EI, you then encourage staff to show the same and lead by example. People will want to work for you and your company if you have high EQ.

Having healthy emotional intelligence allows the individual to have strong social skills. These skills can be developed further with more awareness and practise. These skills are often called "soft skills". Skills like listening, empathy, problem-solving. In my opinion, these skills will become what more employees are looking for in the future.

In fact, a recent survey conducted by non-profit National Association of Colleges and Employers (NACE)[64] included the responses from 260 employers, including both small and large firms like Chevron and IBM. The survey revealed that communication skills ranked in the top three most-sought after qualities by job recruiters.

Another large project, 'Project Oxygen' looked at Google's top managing employees. The results amazed many when the characteristics for success at Google consisted of an array of 'soft skills'. The top five behaviours of Google's best managers were:[65]

1. Is a good coach
2. Empowers team and does not micromanage
3. Creates an inclusive team environment, showing concern for success and well-being
4. Is productive and results-oriented
5. Is a good communicator — listens and shares information

Look at #1 – the top managers are great coaches!

CEOs with high EQ are the future leaders and growers of people and businesses. One of the CEOs who has been identified as showing high EI is Elon Musk, the CEO of Tesla and SpaceX. He has taken it upon himself to work alongside the factory workers in order to build a better understanding of their perspective, therefore, engaging in personal relationships and building empathy. He also recognised there were a high number of injuries in the manufacturing factory and sent out a very descriptive email to all his employees.

> *No words can express how much I care about your safety and wellbeing [sic]. It breaks my heart when someone is injured building cars and trying their best to make Tesla successful.*
>
> *Going forward, I've asked that every injury be reported directly to me, without exception. I'm meeting with the safety team every week and would like to meet every injured person as soon as they are well, so that I can understand from them exactly what we need to do to make it better. I will then go down to the production line and perform the same task that they perform.*
>
> *This is what all managers at Tesla should do as a matter of course. At Tesla, we lead from the front line, not from some safe and comfortable ivory tower. Managers must always put their team's safety above their own.*[66]

It is recognised that not only through Musk's language, but also his actions that he exhibits a high EI.

Another CEO who has been identified as a current leader showing strong EI is former CEO of Pepsi Indra Nooyi. Nooyi states that holding onto an employee is done by "connecting them with the company's business model and what it stands for". She advocates for looking after the employee and valuing them. She says it's important to say, "I value you as a person. I know that you have a life beyond PepsiCo, and I'm going to respect you for your entire life, not just treat you as employee number 4,567." Through her emotional awareness, she has created an environment where the staff feel safe in the knowing that they are cared for and respected.

Richard Branson, founder and chairman of Virgin Group is also recognised as a leader with high EI. He is world-famous for his entrepreneurial ways, and despite his dyslexia, he fought against the stigma and created an empire. He is open about his learning difficulties and is open to sharing his mistakes of the past and how he turned them around, exhibiting strong emotional intelligence.

All of these industry leaders not only show a healthy emotional intelligence, they also show deep gratitude for their workers and are not afraid to show this in public. As well as gratitude, they are constantly asking their employees to generate further information about what could be improved for the team They treat every individual with respect instead of just another 'employee'.[67]

But don't just take my word for it, here's some juicy reports coming out from places like Harvard, TalentSmart and the Empathy Institute.

- Nearly 90% of top performers have a higher level of emotional intelligence.[68]
- Emotional intelligence accounts for 90% of career advancements when two potential employees have similar IQ and technical skills.[69]
- People with high emotional intelligence make $29,000 more, on average, than their counterparts.[70]

EMOTIONAL INTELLIGENCE IS TRAINABLE

Emotional intelligence can be taught and learned. It changes over time. It's not static at all, but it depends on the person's attitude. There are now many incredible programs teaching and developing this skill.

Leading psychologist and lecturer Daniel Goleman became an innovative pioneer of helping bring understanding and context to EQ.[71] His 1995 book, *Emotional Intelligence* was read globally and became a leading authority on how to use and express EQ in the workplace and in all areas of your life.

Daniel Goleman's model of emotional intelligence has been used extensively and he breaks it down into very workable solutions so people can actually learn Emotional Intelligence. He discusses the importance of understanding your own and other's emotions and learning how to motivate and manage yourself.

He uses four easy-to-understand quadrants that I have successfully implemented into my own life and across all business sectors that I have been involved in.

Find out more about your EQ. Download your FREE EQ flyer at **deanpublishing.com/smallsurprises**

THE FOUR QUADRANTS OF EMOTIONAL INTELLIGENCE

1. SELF-AWARENESS

Self-awareness is all about understanding yourself, as the adage says, 'know thyself'. It's about being aware of your own feelings and being inquisitive of your own emotions. For business leaders, being a self-aware leader means to understand your own strengths and weaknesses and not look to cover them up in reactive ways.

We can all build self-awareness by taking time to reflect and assess our own reactions and motives. You can journal things down and ask yourself: *How can I be a better leader? What aspects within myself can I improve? Does my attitude and behaviour lift others up or make them feel inadequate? Do I need to look at my own feelings of self-confidence?*

Everything begins with self-awareness, if you're not aware of your behaviours and reactions, then how can you improve them?

2. SELF-MANAGEMENT

After you have become aware of yourself and your behaviours, self-management allows you to manage them in a healthy and positive way. For example, you may feel annoyance or even anger when someone questions your decisions, but you manage your reaction by not allowing it to rise up and explode. You have the ability to be aware of what is occurring and manage your reaction and the situation. Some people call this 'emotional regulation' – when you learn how to manage and regulate emotions and thoughts that inevitably pop up in business.

A great leader isn't embarrassed to learn self-management techniques. In many ways it leads to self-discipline. Developing self-discipline coupled with awareness is a very helpful skills for any leader.

3. SOCIAL AWARENESS

Once you have mastered yourself, it's important to take these reflections and put them into practise with others. How do you connect, communicate, show empathy and listen to others? Can you sense the level of engagement with people and feel attuned to non-verbal cues?

Do you consider the feelings and responses of others? The ability to empathise and maintain sensitivity of other's moods and emotions allows us to recognise how others may be feeling or perceiving. Examples of good social recognition is empathy and understanding, appreciation and listening. Listening is so important. Kindness and respect are really important too.

Some companies are now using EQ tests for recruiting new team members. They're not only hiring people for their technical skill anymore, they're hiring on emotional intelligence — on how they're going to relate to other people on the team, how are they going to relate to customers, and work together while maintaining empathy and great leadership.

4. SOCIAL MANAGEMENT

Social management includes how you socially manage a team and use those interpersonal skills to generate results. Good social management skills fosters collaboration and connection and increases development and growth. It's all about group development. It's about managing relationships in the best way for everyone.

For example, it includes building friendships, making time for people, caring about people, finding out what's important to them, especially with your team members. Getting to know a bit about their families, knowing what their interests are, knowing about their children — what school they go to — or things they enjoy to do. It's about knowing their favoured skillset and helping people work their genius in a way that supports growth and helps everyone flourish.

Team bonding activities and open discussions foster great social engagement and helps manage it in a way that is inclusive and supportive.

REFLECTION

You will notice that a lot of the emotionally intelligent leaders take time to reflect and think. To observe before reacting.

Utilising personal time for self-reflection is the beginning, then incorporating that into reflection about the team dynamics, the business and the community at large, becomes a natural stepping stone.

Without reflection and contemplation you won't recognise ways you and your team can improve.

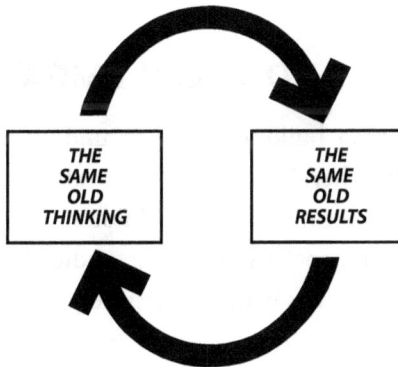

THE SAME OLD THINKING

THE SAME OLD RESULTS

STRESS MANAGEMENT

Stress Management is critical in both your personal life and in the workforce. By having an ability to self-manage you can alter and regulate your stress levels. Poorly managed stress levels affect your ability to focus, make decisions and think clearly.

Social recognition helps with stress too because it helps resolve any types of conflict. It quickly cuts out any conflict in the workplace because you're more open to communication and progress, you don't build a culture of sweeping it under the carpet. If you take time to use emotional intelligence, you'll treat situations and people far better. You'll provide the new type of leadership we are building — conscious and caring leadership. And this type of leadership will change the way we do business and the world.

WHAT HUMANS DO BEST

Humans do something that no robot or animal can do — we make conscious leadership decisions on behalf of bettering the whole. We can access an innate wisdom and act emotionally intelligent (if we foster that skill).

Despite our fast-moving world, robots and automation can't show you authentic heartfelt kindness. They can't relate to your human behaviour and empathise with your emotion.

We must advance in our business technology and growth without losing sight of the innate skills that give us a true sense of belonging and unity.

UNDERSTAND AND SHOW EMPATHY

Empathy is an essential building block to understanding life, it helps us understand each other's strengths and weaknesses and helps build strong workplaces and communities. Children that develop empathy early in life enjoy better social skills in their adult life and they become more active in treating others with kindness, respect and understanding.[72]

According to the authors of *Born for Love: Why Empathy Is Essential-and Endangered* Maia Szalavitz and renowned psychiatrist Bruce Perry say that, "Empathy underlies virtually everything that makes society work — like trust, altruism, collaboration, love, charity. Failure to empathise is a key part of most social problems — crime, violence, war, racism, child abuse, and inequity, to name a few."[73]

For society and the business leaders within it to function at its optimal potential, people must be able to empathise with the plight of others and support each other to ease those challenges. Empathy can be a great driving force for actioning change.

Despite the mounting evidence that shows empathy is truly necessary for individual and business success, it seems the lack of empathy is becoming more common than ever before.

A study of nearly 14,000 college students found that students today have about 40% less empathy than college kids had in the 1980s and 1990s.[74] Internationally recognised educational psychologist and author Michele Borba[75] believes that the loss of empathy is one of the chief reasons why so many kids are struggling with pressure and mental health.

Geelong Grammar School recognised this early and developed a culture of positive education. They have set up a whole department and train not only their students and teachers, but also other schools and parents. I believe that building empathy and a positive mental attitude in early employment training will be vital for future employment.

It's been suggested that the rapid advancement of technology, increased populations, and general trends towards less community involvement has reduced our human interactions and therefore limited our empathetic concerns for each other.

On the upside, empathy is wonderful for reducing divisions and boundaries. It acts as bridge for people to bond and share their feelings. However, some people do lack empathy or have an empathy deficient disorder. They may feel good on their own but they lack empathy for others and have poor social skills.

Positive education is important to help the business world become more empathetic. To understand that care belongs in business not just in homes.

Professor Liliana Bove from the University of Melbourne is an expert on this subject. She featured in a fantastic online article in *Pursuit* titled 'Is Empathy Good for Business?'[76] In short, she outlines that:

"Empathy is definitely good for business."

Professor Bove says, "Empathy is a key factor for businesses because it communicates care for clients."

In short, empathy can:

• boost sales
• enhance customer satisfaction
• increase consumer compliance
• Improve brand perception
• Enable innovation

She says, "Salespeoples' customer-oriented attitudes and behaviour is strengthened when their empathy is high. An empathetic salesperson can read what type of relationship the customer expects and desires."[77]

Many places that promote empathy also have happier and healthier employees. Professor Bove says, "High-empathy service professionals like doctors, nurses, teachers or social workers are likely to experience more positive emotions, like pleasure and warmth, as patients and clients' express relief and gratitude. In turn, this brings higher job satisfaction. Related evidence shows that high empathy trait is associated with lower burnout."[78]

Being too empathetic however isn't the answer, research concludes that a balanced and natural amount of empathy is healthier than over-the-top self-sacrificing empathy. Too much empathy predisposes others to become less productive and it can lead to burnt-out.

SKILLS OF THE FUTURE

With the rise of automation, AI and robotics, human relationships will become more needed than ever. Emotional Intelligence, empathy and care are innately human and we will always crave this human connection. Though I love evolution and innovation, this doesn't solely belong in the area of technology. We as humans must also evolve and become better in the way we behave, lead and communicate.

I believe our human skills will be the more sought-after asset than just the skill itself. There might be 1000 engineers but who is the engineer that can talk to somebody in a language they understand, and still be a fantastic engineer? Who is the engineer that can make a company understand why that specific shape bridge is stronger and safer than the others?

Sure, qualifications and skill requirements are still needed, but who has the adaptable skills? Who has the soft skills coupled with the technical skills? Who can communicate their skill to others and embrace a team's diversity?

It's no longer only about whether you're a generalist or a specialist type but if you also possess those human connection skills.

THE EVOLUTION OF THE EMPLOYEE

← Past	Future →
Work 9-5	Work anytime
Work in a corporate office	Work anywhere
Use company equipment	Use any device
Focused on inputs	Focused on outputs
Climb the corporate ladder	Create your own ladder
Pre-defined work	Customize work
Hoards information	Shares information
No voice	Staff encouraged to give advice
Relies on email	Relies on collaboration technologies
Focused on knowledge	Focused on adaptive learning
Corporate learning and teaching	Democratized learning and teaching

We know now that in 20 years' time, many jobs won't be around. But there are also growth areas, like the service, tourism and health industries where the power is in the people. Yes, you have machines, yes you may even have a robot as your personal trainer, but it's not customer service, it's not building a rapport. It's not heartfelt emotion or compassion.

Yes, you want a personal trainer to drive you hard but they have got to have empathy too. They have got to know when to push you hard and when not to. They have to know what drives you from within to get the best out of you. And the same goes in business, those deeper skills that involve a level of emotional intelligence will become more important than ever.

Even if you're going to a supermarket, and you've got your hands full and a couple of children yelling for your attention, sometimes you just want a cashier (a person) to do that job for you. You really don't want to go through the self-serve and juggle everything. As much as people like the convenience, there's a lot of people that prefer a person.

Especially when you're making decisions. A lot of people buy clothes online but you can't feel the fabric or know the exact cut. Of course, you may do your research online to get better information but some people still want to try it on then and there.

If people fail to develop their emotional intelligence, even if it's slightly uncomfortable for them, the future will belong to those who have the skill and the EQ to adapt to today's diverse world.

WHO WILL IT BE?

So who will be most successful? What type of person will succeed in the future?

If we look at the broad range of future areas we will notice one thing in particular. That regardless of the industry, the pace of change will be a major factor. Think of these fields as examples:

- Internet of Things
- Health care
- Security and privacy
- Drones and autonomous vehicles

- Artificial Intelligence and software bots
- Automation
- Mobile apps for communications, collaboration and reporting
- Robotics in manufacturing and service
- Social media communications
- Online learning

How fast are these areas evolving? Exceptionally quick.

Business evolution occurs more rapidly each year and new specialised fields emerge every year. This means that new skills will also emerge and therefore new styles of employees will be needed. For example, what do these jobs have in common? App developer, drone operator, content creator, driverless car engineer, social media manager, data scientist, podcaster, AI chatbot writer, cloud architect.

They all only emerged in the last ten years.

So, what type of new jobs will be created in the next 10 or 20 years? Many we probably haven't even heard of yet. One report from 2016 suggests that 65% of children who are now entering primary school will end up working in jobs that we don't even know exist right now.[79]

Though the idea of a generalist or specialist has been traditionally acceptable and debated vigorously, those two concepts also support an older system of business; futurists suggest a new style will inevitably emerge. Although we will always need specialists, especially in fields like medicine and health, we also need specialists to have a good general idea of how their specialisation effects other areas.

WHAT IS A SPECIALIST?

Specialists focus on one specific job area in a particular industry or market. Their knowledge is specific but very deep. Specialists thrive in companies that hire them to be the expert, the highly-skilled professional in a chosen field.

A specialist is often considered an I-shaped person. They have a single specialty and don't know an extensive amount about different areas. The letter "I" represents their deep knowledge and experience in one area.

I-shaped people can succeed in many environments, but typically not in professions requiring intensive cross-collaboration and a broad range of skills.

D
E
P
T
H

I-SHAPED PERSON

WHAT IS A GENERALIST?

Generalists are often called a *jack of all trades*. They don't have the deep focus on one subject like the specialists but the generalist's strength is being knowledgeable about all the moving parts of an industry. Generalists have a broad knowledge base that is very helpful to the whole. Generalists know something about everything but not everything about something. For example, on a soccer sporting team, a generalist would be able to fill in for many positions, but maybe not be specialised in one specific position.

BASE KNOWLEDGE/SKILLS

GENERALIST PERSON

THE COMBINED SPECIALIST AND GENERALIST

In 1991 a man called David Guest wrote an article for *The Independent* in London called "The hunt is on for the Renaissance Man of computing." He coined the term "T-shape" to describe someone with *both* generalist and specialist skills.[80]

This idea became further popularised when Tim Brown, CEO of design firm IDEO, revealed the type of people he wanted to work for his large organisation. He said when recruiting, his company base their decisions on the breadth *and* depth of experience. This term is a new type of employee, it's referred to as a "deep generalist".

A "T-shaped" person has deep expertise like a specialist but has the added breadth to expand out into other disciplines. The broad experience in different disciplines is the top horizontal bar and the deep expertise in their field is represented by the "I" vertical bar, like the "I" is specialist.

Computer scientist Jim Spohrer from IBM encouraged T-shaped professionals for his team's development and many other tech giants believe that T-shaped people are the better collaborative innovators of which the industry needs to cultivate to stay on top and in touch with society's needs.

A 2016 research article found that teams utilising the T-model principles performed better during uncertain times. Some T-shaped examples are people in management roles or content marketers.[81]

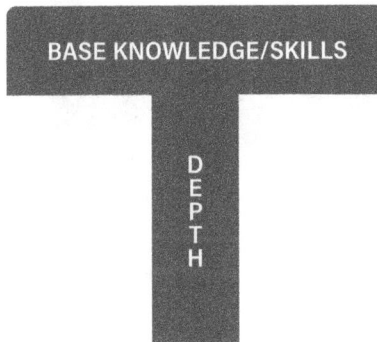

T-SHAPED PERSON

PI SHAPED PEOPLE

The Pi shaped people are also a new style of employee. They have a broad general base but also two separate areas of deep expertise, creating a shape similar to the symbol for Pi.

Ashley Friedlein, the CEO of Econsultancy wrote an article highlighting the new type of person required for the future. He said "We used to talk about T-shaped people, who were marketers with a broad set of knowledge and skills in marketing but deep specialism in a particular area. But I've started talking about pi-shaped (π) people. These are marketers with a broad base of knowledge in all areas, but capabilities in both 'left brain' and 'right brain' disciplines. They are both analytical and data-driven, yet understand brands, storytelling and experiential marketing."[82]

A job example of a pi-shaped person could be a person with two specialities that work well together and give them a broad range of knowledge, for example:

a product designer + coder

a musician + producer

a writer + web analytics

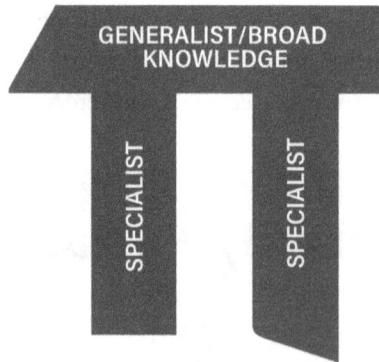

PI-SHAPED PERSON

COMB-SHAPED PEOPLE

Comb shaped employees have a broad range of knowledge *and* multiple areas of expertise which gives the shape of a comb. The columns of specialty however are not too deep and obviously not as long as an "I shape". However, as the world accelerates and has a whole new emergence of interconnectivity, multiple areas with sufficient depth can often be more valuable than being a solitary specialist.

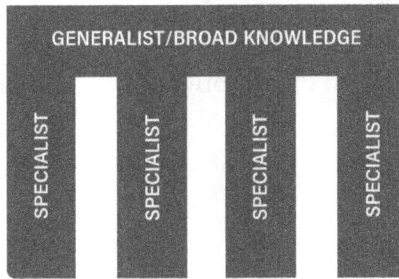

COMB-SHAPED PERSON

E-SHAPED PEOPLE

Gaurav Sharma wrote a great LinkedIn article perfectly capturing the 'E-shaped' style of employee. He said, "Expertise in few areas, Experience across several areas, specialist with proven execution skills and Explorative minds combined to form E shaped employee. However, a lot of emphases is placed on the E: execution. E-shaped people translate ideas into reality. Employees and teams who are willing to explore in order to satisfy their curiosity, and who will be taking the risks to execute new ideas and innovate, will be highly in demand in near future."[83]

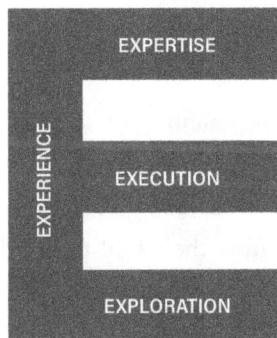

E-SHAPED PERSON

THE PROBLEM WITH ALL THESE "TYPES"

Though in the business world, generalists and specialists both have their strengths and weaknesses, they only focus on the 'seen skillsets'.

But the issue is it leaves out two critical areas: **environment and emotional intelligence.**

A 2018 study looked at the pace of change by using the impact of the Soviet Union's collapse on the performance of theoretical mathematicians as an experiment, the study showed the more *general* scientists performed best when the pace of change was slower. But the *expert* specialists gained advantage when the pace of change increased.[84]

The study went on to suggests that two types of deeper capabilities can improve creative performance whether you're a generalist or specialist.

1. The ability to *connect* ideas across subject areas.
2. The ability to efficiently build on progress in your field and seize opportunities emerging at the *frontier of change.*[85]

In other words, being able to move with the times and still connect and innovate will be vital. As Charles Darwin said, "It is not the strongest or the most intelligent who will survive but those who can best manage change."

> **The person that can innovate, adapt and connect will be the workplace superstar.
> It will take an emotionally intelligent person to combine these skills effectively.**

Skills of course will be always be essential, but whether you're a T-shape, I-shape or Pi-shape you must be able to *transition yourself for the future.*

This is because businesses will evolve rapidly and people will need adaptable attitudes and skillsets. Businesses will be upskilling their staff and adapting to the rapid social changes. Businesses will be implementing new technologies and training their staff to use them.

For example, Amazon just announced that it will invest US$700 million to retrain 100,000 employees in new technologies[86] – that's a third of its U.S. workforce.

But Amazon aren't alone. Other big businesses see the value in training their staff — many are providing training for people to increase their "soft skills".

As Amazon said, "A look at how our workforce has changed over time helps us understand the impact of technology on the labor market and highlights the need for both more technical skills and an always-learning mindset."[87]

In other words, Amazon is investing is teaching their employees more about future technology and more about how to have a *learning mindset to embrace it.*

Are we entering a never-seen-before-era, where a new type of leader emerges? I think so.

Workplace change is inevitable. More and more people are working in the gig economy, more are working flexible hours and using a myriad of technology. We must have a learning mindset. We must realise that this learning mindset never stops. Whether you're the CEO, the cleaner, the computer analyst or the clerk. Learn for a lifetime. Einstein said, "The greatest scientists are artists as well."

It seems combining skills and emotional intelligence will give people the edge.

> *"The shift to lifelong learning is absolutely essential. As the pace of technological change quickens, we need to be sure that employees are keeping up with the right skills to thrive in the Fourth Industrial Revolution. That applies to both technical and soft skills. There will be changes in both areas."*
>
> *— Zvika Krieger,*
> *Head of Technology Policy and Partnerships,*
> *Center for the Fourth Industrial Revolution,*
> *World Economic Forum*

Make a shift to lifelong learning. Look at your business and personal skillset from a lifelong view. Take a bird's eye view.

DO AN ADAPTIVE INVENTORY ON YOURSELF AND YOUR SKILLSET

Ask yourself:

- *Am I adapting?*

- *Is the business adapting?*

- *Am I increasing my soft skills/EQ?*

- *Are my team trained in soft skills and EQ?*

- *Am I increasing my skillset for the future?*

- *Is the team increasing their skillset for the future?*

- *Am I improving?*

- *Are we improving?*

- *Does the business revenue reflect these improvements?*

- *Am I future-proofing my business?*

- *Am I future-proofing our team?*

Download a FREE Adaptive Inventory template at **deanpublishing.com/smallsurprises**

PART FOUR

LEADERSHIP OF THE FUTURE

"A boss has the title, a leader has the people."

Simon Sinek

COMMUNITY LEADERSHIP AND GLOBAL LEADERSHIP
THE POWER OF COMMUNITY IN BUSINESS (AND LIFE)

Businesses are at the heart of each community. Where would you be without your local grocer or petrol station? People often overlook how important businesses are to our sense of unity and belonging.

I challenge business owners of all sizes to ensure their entire community benefits from their involvement and leadership. You do this by continuing to grow and develop your business and your people. You create more jobs and develop more economic benefit for your region, your employees and the economy.

It doesn't matter whether you're the local farmer or an international media mogul – if your community doesn't benefit from your business and leadership within the community then you're not maximising your impact or your influence.

Small businesses are the heart and soul of the community. When it thrives, so does the community. I challenge businesses to improve their community in some way. I encourage owners to go out and actively grow and develop their community and improve people's lives.

Even if you're classified as a "global business" it doesn't mean that you can't think locally too. You have a duty of care to your community to show what global and local leadership looks like.

We often see sporting stars return to their local high school once they've hit the big time. They remember their roots and want to give back to their humble community. They teach the local kids about their sport and often encourage them to go for their dreams.

Business leaders should do the same.

There are so many ways businesses can contribute to their community. It can be as small as sponsoring the local sporting clubs to as big as hiring local people when you can. If you open any business book these days, most are talking about global and international business deals. Now, don't get me wrong – I also think globally and want you to expand exponentially, however, I think our corporate social responsibility (CSR) is to also lift others up as we grow, and this means not forgetting where you came from and not forgetting as you rise high, you can also lift your local community.

If you have the capacity to improve the community, or even a single person's life by being a better business person, use it. Not everyone has that privilege.

You can still have the world's best practice or business. You can still have the best product. But you can do that by building your community too.

Think about your local suppliers before you head for the cheapest deal from overseas. Check out the opportunities under your nose and see if you could hire a local teenager in need of some part time work.

One example of both international and local leadership models is the Rotary Club (rotary.org). For over 110 years Rotary and its network of over 1.2 million people have created change in communities all over the world. Though they are an international organisation, they don't overlook real problems that exist in their communities.

And what many people don't realise is that you may already be a local leader and not even realise the impact you have. Sport coaches, teachers, local business owners, parents within the community all play a role in building the community culture.

As Bill Gates said, "As we look ahead into the next century, leaders will be those who empower others."

THE NEW MODEL OF BUSINESS

I encourage business owners to see their business in a new way. In fact, I ask them to deliberately see their business entirely differently by seeking out opportunities to impact and benefit their community through their involvement. I often ask my clients to get out within their town and start to know the people and businesses, not only do they get an abundance of referrals, but they start to understand the needs of their neighbours and people.

You will build trust and get to know the local plumber and builder, the local grocer and butcher. You'll engage within the community and people will begin to trust you and your business.

I travel overseas often, and when I go to places like France and Italy, I want to eat the local foods and experience their regional wines. It's really exciting because when you're travelling, you're experiencing something unique and local. It's a bona-fide experience of their culture and way of life. In Australia, this regional thinking is only starting to be explored and I think it's a step in the right direction. A new way of doing business is to be proudly local – even if you're importing overseas you can be proudly local as well.

If you're a restaurant owner in a wonderful region and you're not serving local food and wine, then you're missing out on good business. Some pretend they're doing it but they don't really understand the dynamics of it. For example, you may have seen the simple French jam called Bonne Maman. They began in a small town nestled in the heart of South West France and are now found in over 100 countries in major food stores. Why would so many countries want this jam? It's just jam, right? There is jam in every country. Why would people want this jam more than others? Well it's because it's sold as a traditional and authentic French jam. They're sold in little glass jars from the same region it began in and people love an authentic experience. They'll pay more for it because it means more. Bonne Maman means 'grandmother' in French. Now, who doesn't want an authentic motherly homegrown jam to spread on their toast or croissant?

The point of course isn't about the jam, it's about the experience. It's about the feeling of having something homemade and authentic. What's better – packet pasta from the supermarket or homemade pasta made by an Italian grandmother from her traditional recipe?

We all have our little formula for success.

So, what makes you and your business authentic? What is special about your region? How could your leadership or business improve your community?

The well-known mantra "think globally, act locally" became increasingly popularised with climate change, however its origins began in town planning with its view to build 'cities of evolution'.

The business world has also caught onto this catch-cry and looked at its methods in terms of production and impact. In a bid to try and combine both global and local thinking, some companies used the term 'glocal' – a combination of the words 'global' and 'local'. It has been said that Akio Morita, the founder of Sony was the catalyst of using this term in the business world, using 'glocal' in advertising and branding strategies throughout the '80s and '90s.

Now numerous businesses refer to themselves as GLOCAL.

I'm all for ACTING locally. Whether you are a local business or an international powerhouse, you can still lift your community and people to new heights of success. This is not just a preference but an amazing business model.

A lot of the big companies do this very thing. For example, IKEA in China sell smaller beds than they do in the USA. Their houses and people want smaller – they may have a global business but they look at the local people. McDonalds hire local teenagers and even alter their menu in some countries to meet their local preferences. For example, in India they offer a vegetarian and curried alternative to burgers, and in some other countries they offer noodles and spaghetti to adapt to each specific culture.

LOCAL	GLOBAL	GLOCAL
Thinking Locally, Acting Locally	Thinking Globally, Acting Globally	Thinking Globally, Acting Locally

This business model can easily Delight, Disrupt and Deliver! How do I know? It's the one I have successfully used my whole business career. And now it's the one I help my clients use to grow and build their empires. It works.

WHAT BUSINESS ARE YOU REALLY IN?

Now, in business you'll hear a lot of people say, "Find your niche, discover your unique selling point." I agree, but a lot of the time, people get that wrong. They think they're in a certain business but they're not. Often, they're simply stuck in an old mindset and no one has challenged it.

When I bought a run-down conference centre in Woodend and started to develop it, the first thing I did was become involved in the community. I made sure that I got to know the local business networking groups and the local suppliers. There was no tourism board locally — so along with some wineries and other food places in the Macedon Ranges area, we started the Macedon Ranges tourism board. We grew and developed that including all the other tourism and businesses in the local area. But we also tried to educate other business owners and tell them what industry they were actually in. They were in the tourism industry, even the local butcher.

The butcher said, "Oh, we're not in tourism, we're a butcher. We sell meat."

I said, "Who is your biggest client?"

And they said, "Well, you guys at Campaspe House."

And I said, "Well, what do we do?"

"Tourism." The butcher said.

"So, you're in tourism."

Indirectly tourism is part of the fabric of many regions which are growing and developing. And the same with the wine industry, which is more obvious. And all those industries that provide tourism businesses or are indirectly influenced by tourism, are in tourism. That community involvement is vital because when you're putting back into the community, you're also getting to be known, liked and trusted. If they trust you, they'll do business with you. And being involved in the community helps build that trust.

Now, on top of being involved in the community and creating the local tourism bureau, we'd also look after people who were a point of call for the tourists. When we first started, we would make hot scones and take them down to the Information Centre and give them to the people who were working there. Sometimes, there'd be a paid worker but there were also volunteers. We'd bake some hot scones with jam and cream and deliver it to them in the morning. Now, it cost us next to nothing, it was only a 5-minute drive down the road, but guess who they talked about all day? When tourists came in and said, "Where do we eat? Where do we stay? What do we visit?" Our business was front of mind because we delivered some nice hot scones that morning and they felt a bit special because no one else did that. It was such a simple thing to do and they thought, "Okay, what can I do for them... I will give them business."

Now of course, we had great brochures and did tours and meals etc, but it was those simple things that made a difference in the community. Over time we became an icon within the Macedon Ranges area, so if there were any visiting press or special guests coming to the area, the local council and other people would send them to us.

And the same with the wineries, because we only served local wine and food, some of our best clients and referrals came from our suppliers. We looked after them and they looked after us.

Now, it doesn't matter if you have a business in the city or the country – we used the same techniques and they work regardless of location. Because it's all about the experience. You're selling experiences. People want to have a great experience, they want to be involved. They want to meet the locals. They want to eat where the locals eat. They don't want to be caught in the tourist trap.

THE HEARTBEAT OF A COMMUNITY

As I've mentioned, I came from a farming family and though I went out into the big, wide world and became a successful business man, I was lucky enough to keep in contact with our local community. I thank my mother for leading by example.

Growing up in a farming community many things revolved around our local sporting groups, our local school and our local church. Everybody went to church back in those days. In many ways, you were expected to get involved in the community. So, if you weren't playing football, you'd help out in other ways, perhaps at the local dances or community fairs.

I got to witness my parents' involvement in the different groups they belonged to or contributed to. Mum started the local Scout group and ran that for a number of years. She was President of the Country Women's Association as well as President of the golf club. She was always in a leadership role and giving back to the greater community. Despite some terrible personal traumas, my mum sought refuge within her various roles and built incredible leadership skills. She was never a victim. Her positive mindset and engagement within the community showed me the value of contribution. She was a powerhouse in the community and she was a role model for being a local changemaker.

As I got older and went to boarding school at The Geelong College, I continued to witness the power of community. We were all encouraged to get involved in local activities. I joined the choir and band and did musical productions as well as played sport. Although I wasn't particularly good at sport, I discovered hockey and became quite good at it. I enjoyed playing tennis too.

The school was great in making sure we were involved in local activities. And even as I got older and went to the Australian National University, once again, I got involved. I became Treasurer of the Burgmann College and organised various activities. Yes, I was there to study but community involvement was in my blood and getting to know other people made a positive difference in my life. I created a fantastic network of friends because I was involved in so many different things. This community spirit remained within me and became the business model I understood and worked with.

Now, I have mentioned these things not because I want to ramble on about my extra activities but because it did something more than involve me in my community. It made a huge difference to my life and gave me leadership and team skills along the way.

Naturally, at the time, I didn't even realise that I was building them, but in reflection – it was all these activities and community-based programs which helped shape my character.

Whether you're the local soccer coach or the local owner of an apple orchard – your role within the community is much more significant than your occupation. You're a leader. Even if you don't formally classify yourself as one, if you're contributing to the greater community, *you are a leader.*

> *"No leader sets out to be a leader. People set out to live their lives, expressing themselves fully. When that expression is of value, they become leaders. So the point is not to become a leader. The point is to become yourself, to use yourself completely – all your skills, gifts and energies – in order to make your vision manifest. You must withhold nothing. You must, in sum, become the person you started out to be, and to enjoy the process of becoming."*
>
> *— Warren Bennis*

LOCAL BECOMES GLOBAL

I want to tell you about a twelve-year-old girl from Uruguay called Victoria Alonsoperez. Back in 2001 Victoria saw how the outbreak of the Foot-and-Mouth disease devastated her country and killed an unprecedented amount of cattle. She started wondering if she could design a monitoring system to track the cattle's behaviour and detect the disease early. Fast-forward 11 years later and while working at university she heard of a competition that could develop young people's innovative ideas. She entered the competition and won.

Victoria became the founder and inventor of a revolutionary system Chipsafer. And yes, you guessed it, this helps farmers track their livestock's behaviour to detect issues. Her technology also supplies important data to support sustainable farming practises.

Victoria went on to become an engineer and receive an incredible amount of global awards for her invention and innovative solution. But let's not forget where this originated from: one girl's idea to help her community.

I am all for local awards too. You're never too big to enter a local award, nor ever too small to enter a local award. Local awards show a mark of recognition and respect for your community.

One year, Campaspe House won a huge amount of awards: Business of the Year, the Food and Beverage Award, the Customer Service Award, and a Tourism Business Award; out of 10 awards we won seven of them. That was both embarrassing and memorable because we worked really hard to be a community business that people loved.

But because each section was judged by different judges we knew we were judged on our merits. Funny enough, 15 years later, that moment is still talked about in the community. Communities themselves feel pride. This is beautiful.

I have also spent some years being a judge during the Tourism Awards which is a lovely honour to be involved with. What I have noticed time and time again is that the awards often go to those who include a little wow factor that you're not expecting or are pleasantly surprised by. A local attribute or niche that has been highlighted to benefit the entire community not just a business.

When I get asked about achieving local or state awards, I tell people my method: We concentrated on 3 key areas: *marketing, business development, and team development.*

We focused on these areas first and foremost. We marketed our business so people knew it existed. We developed the business so it could support growth without compromising quality and we developed a high-performance team that was customer-centric.

We got local people and governing bodies involved, including local media and publicity. Again, never overlook the importance of your local media, they are tremendous advocates for you. You can use feature pieces or editorials to help market and promote your business locally and use on your website too.

We developed relationships with local suppliers, businesses and individuals. We went that extra mile as a general rule, not an exception. That made all the difference.

Now, when you receive an award – be proud of it. Stand up in the community as a proud local winner. Add any of your award successes to your email signatures, brochures, website and social media platforms and don't forget to refer to them during new business proposals or when preparing or submitting quotes.

You see, these local awards give your business credibility and social proof that you provide a superior product or service. These types of stories attract local journalists, writers and other media to your award-winning business.

We all know that potential clients and customers want the reassurance of third-party endorsements when they are looking for services or products. Local awards give that endorsement without you having to do it.

BUILDING COMMUNITY LEADERS

It has been shown that when leaders collaborate and engage the community, the quality of life improves for those communities.[88] Therefore, if you don't feel that you're a leader – then support those who are leaders. According to many reports, engaged citizens are the backbone of flourishing communities. Communities with strong local leaders have a better influence on social issues, such as lower crime rates, and betterment of education. So, what has this got to do with business? Everything!

Research from the *Journal of Business Ethics* showed that ethical values related to the level of corporate social responsibility and to the amount a company contributed to the sustainable development of the community. In simpler terms, people with community-minded business ethics played a major role in developing their community.

We can't overlook this, nor should we. In fact, it must be brought to the fore. CSR must be valued in a way that breeds more conscious business leaders and creates better and more sustainable businesses for the future.

We need to coach our leaders to grow more leaders. As Bill Gates said, "Everyone needs a coach. It doesn't matter whether you're a basketball player, a tennis player, a gymnast or a bridge player."[89]

I feel the same.

I imagine all the mistakes I could have avoided if I had a great business mentor early on in my career. Everyone needs someone to work with them and bounce ideas off. As I mentioned ealier, when I was horse-riding, there were four or five people that were coaching me to be a better rider. Now, even though there were better riders than me, I managed to ride at elite level in Australia at national level against the Olympic riders. Those Olympic riders became friends of mine but also clients. The reason I became better quickly was because of their elite coaching. I had experts show me what to avoid and what to train. It saved me years of trial and error.

I wish I knew the power of coaching when I first started in business. When I first began in business, I learnt by making a lot of mistakes. If only I'd had a business mentor or a business coach to help me develop my business, I would have got there much faster, made less mistakes and built a bigger and better business. But back then, it never occurred to me. In fact, business coaching was in its infancy. Now, business coaching is much more recognised and easily accessible. It's not unusual anymore.

But I still think coaching someone in their business should be the same as coaching a high-performance athlete. You enter into the relationship with a big goal and intention. Not just a 'see how it goes' attitude.

This may sound a bit much to some people, but I even offer a guarantee to my clients. Depending on the type of business they have

I guarantee that they will get their money back (so whatever I cost will come back to them in increased business revenue) and sometimes I guarantee a three-fold or even ten-fold return depending on the effort they put in too. I'm not afraid of this guarantee – I thrive in it because I know I can show business owners how to grow their businesses and increase revenue. I'm not a spectator. I want to get involved and do a good job. It's what I love to do. It's my why.

I get out of bed every morning to work with talented business owners, to inspire them to make positive and simple changes in their business and personal lives. I involve myself in their business in a way to help shape their future. I want them to minimise risks and avoid mistakes that cost them time, team and money. And in doing that, it allows these businesses to get on a positive growth track, create more local jobs and, as a result, build stronger local communities and positively impact lives simultaneously.

This is why I get out of bed and do what I do. Money is the by-product of doing this well but it's not the primary motivation.

What is your why?
Why do you get out of bed and do what you do?

Take a moment to really think about it. To dig deep and find your deepest reason for doing what you do.

It's quite phenomenal that when you know the reason you do what you do, your motivation lifts and your energy rises. You become more engaged and stop going through the motions.

This happened to a client of mine recently. Let's call him Geoff. After we went through a coaching session about Geoff's real WHY, he immediately changed. He had a light-bulb moment and 'got it'. He realised that his small local business wasn't running just to bring in a profit each month but that he was providing a service much needed in the community. A service that he was passionate about and the reason he had kept at it for over 20 years.

Geoff rang me recently; he was all excited because his sales within the last two months exceeded what they had done in the past 6 months. This didn't surprise me, but it surprised Geoff.

In fact, Geoff is very similar to many business owners that I work with, his business was already well and truly established, 22 years to be precise, but it had been sitting on the same revenue for years. It was performing well but remained the same each year. He needed to get some new strategies and understand how to grow.

We started on some small issues, understanding the financials, doing better quotes, following up on their quotes and having systems in place. We did some sales training but just with some small tweaks in the right direction, sales went through the roof and their conversion rate doubled. They started to feel that they didn't need to discount at all.

Though we worked on some typical business strategies for growth, Geoff's personal levels of enjoyment also grew – he knew why he did what he did. He wanted to increase his sales and give more people jobs and help more local community groups. He began to expand his business, his mindset and the impact it had within the community.

That's the power of a business owner ignited from within and acting in the best interests of building a sustainable business.

"Leadership is a potent combination of strategy and character. But if you must be without one, be without the strategy."

— Norman Schwarzkopf

❖ **7 CORE PRINCIPLES** ❖

FOR BUILDING LOCAL/GLOCAL BUSINESSES AND LEADERSHIP

1. Get involved
2. Think about positive impacts you can have within your community
3. Lift up the leaders and doers in the community
4. Build a business that also serves your community
5. Know your why and share it with your customers/ community
6. Support local suppliers/producers/workers
7. Grow your business to maximise your impact

THERE'S NO SMALL THING

"It is better to lead from behind and to put others in front, especially when you celebrate victory when nice things occur. You take the front line when there is danger. Then people will appreciate your leadership."

— *Nelson Mandela*

Richard Branson said, "A big business, starts small." I agree!

Everything great begins small. Every great person, every great business. Don't be afraid to use the power of small surprises, of small gestures, of small ideas and grow them.

This is how you can DELIGHT, DISRUPT and DELIVER.

It sounds simple I know but from my personal experience the small things make the big things. Like a bullseye on a dart board, that tiny point makes the whole game.

Nothing is too tiny to make a difference. A smile makes a difference. A kind word. A caring gesture. Business is a whole bunch of small things done right.

In Australia, 96% of businesses are small businesses with less than twenty employees.[90] Now when you think about it, that's a huge majority. Together, small business is one mighty powerful sector.

Though some people think they're small, they really aren't. In fact, I know some people who invited their local hairdresser to their wedding — that hairdresser isn't just someone small to them, it's their friend. I got to know many local business owners and I can tell you right now, many of us still keep in touch and get together. That's not a small thing. That's a lifelong big deal.

A leader is a leader. Whether someone leads a community sports team, a National business franchise or the state of Victoria — leadership is critical for change to occur.

See a video of Milton in action '5 Ways In Action'. Go to **deanpublishing.com/smallsurprises**

⚜ YOU DIDN'T COME THIS FAR ⚜
TO ONLY COME THIS FAR.

Don't just put this book down and walk away. Make a positive change today. Download any of my free tools and begin to grow yourself and your business.

Nothing shifts until you make a decision to change something. So, take this moment and know you can transform your business and grow it exponentially with a few very easy and simple tools – done right!

ABOUT THE AUTHOR

Milton Collins is the principal of The Action Business Coach. He is a certified business coach and a qualified Accountant who is committed to empowering clients with simple yet effective tools to manage and achieve their business and personal goals. Milton has an arsenal of knowledge and application developed over 40 years in business. He has won numerous awards for business excellence and is in high demand for his knowledge and experience.

With a career spanning across several industries, Milton is a commercially astute business executive accustomed to executing a hands-on approach. With his exceptional leadership skills and broad-based commercial acumen, Milton's approach to business has resulted in major business success. His ability to identify business needs, along with his extensive knowledge in financial management, business administration and business evaluation, has seen Milton transform businesses successfully.

Milton grew up on a farm where his career and love for horses started at a young age learning to ride, helping with the stud cattle, working on the wheat property, and doing his part in the family business. A normal childhood for any country boy before he went off to boarding school in Geelong. But it's what Milton did with this that turned his life around.

Whilst attending the Australian National University, Milton taught riding at the main horse-riding Centre in Canberra, where he later became the Chief Instructor and Manager. This got several firms interested in Milton, as not only was he qualified now, he also had working experience and had built a successful business. Not many graduates had this type of profile at such a young age.

Milton received an offer from PriceWaterhouseCoopers in Melbourne which was a fantastic training ground, but at the same time, Milton was competing at a high level in 3-Day Eventing competitions and found himself needing a balance. He decided to leave PWC and move out of Melbourne where he managed to find a progressive accounting firm in the country.

Milton became one of the 9 Partners and Directors of the RGM Financial Group with over 200 staff, providing taxation and business advice to a wide range of small to medium-sized businesses. His experience and training at PriceWaterhouseCoopers enabled him to excel in this role for over fifteen years.

Next, he was the founding Principal at Collins Ryan, an Accountancy and Business Advisory firm, specialising in providing taxation and business advice to the hospitality, tourism, and equestrian industries.

Later, realising his passion, Milton sold out of his extremely successful accounting firm and purchased Campaspe Country House. Utilising his sought-after skills, he transformed the poorly performing conference centre into a highly acclaimed Country House Hotel, business retreat and fine-dining restaurant. His deep and passionate commitment to excellence and total dedication ensured he delivered the best possible outcome to every one of his stakeholders. It soon became a renowned and awarded tourist destination with a valuation increase from $1.5mill to $6.5mill and an occupancy growth from 45% to 95%. From winning the inaugural Business Excellence Awards in Tourism and Hospitality he and his team at Campaspe Country House went on to be finalists on 10 occasions and winners of 6 Awards including the Telstra Business of the Year. Since selling the business, Milton has continued his involvement with the Business Awards as a mentor, judge and sponsor. He is also currently a judge of The Victorian Tourism Industry Awards.

Recently, Milton Collins was the CEO and General Manager of The Transport Hotel complex, which comprises Taxi Kitchen, Transport Hotel, Transit Rooftop Lounge and Taxi Riverside all located at Federation Square in Melbourne.

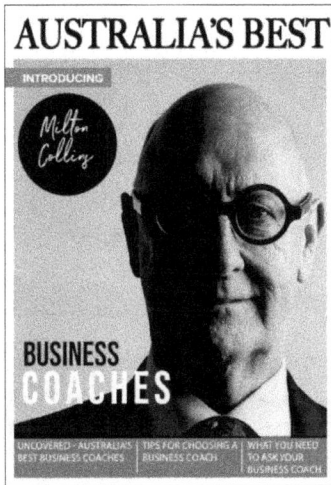

This broad experience has led Milton to his current passion as a sought-after Business Coach with the world's leading coaching firm ActionCOACH®. It's a role in which he has helped hundreds of small business people to meet the challenges and maximise the opportunities of their enterprises.

Milton is no stranger to business, with a proven record of delivering exceptional results in all areas. He possesses an intuitive capacity to identify key drivers and successfully implement plans and strategies, leading many businesses to sustained success.

Along with his busy career in the commercial world, Milton has always followed his passion in the horse industry as a competitive rider and administrator. Competing in equestrian three-day events to advanced level, dressage to advanced level, as well as show jumping and hunting with The Oaklands Hunt Club.

miltoncollins.actioncoach.com

WORK WITH MILTON

I get out of bed every morning to work with talented business owners to inspire them to make positive and simple changes in their business and personal lives so they minimise risk and avoid mistakes. Mistakes that cost them time, energy and money. Doing that then allows those businesses to get on a positive growth track that allows us together to create more local jobs and, as result, build stronger local communities and positively impact lives simultaneously.

Milton is an award-winning business owner with certificatons in the following areas:

DISC | Critical Thinking | EIQ-2 | Learning Styles | Motivators

Assessments 24×7
GLOBAL LEADER IN ASSESSMENT TECHNOLOGY

Action COACH CERTIFIED

INTERNATIONALLY ACCREDITED ADVANCED CERTIFIED PRACTITIONER #017

Judge
2019 RACV VICTORIAN TOURISM AWARDS

Judge
2021 VICTORIAN TOURISM AWARDS

KEYNOTE TALKS AND WORKSHOPS

- 6 Steps to a Better Business
- 5 Ways to Grow Your Profits
- Are You Driving Your Business, or Is It Driving You?
- Time Rich — How to Use Time to Your Advantage
- Finance Rich — How to Master the Finances in Your Business
- Phone Rich – How to Make Your Phone a Profit Centre
- Service Rich – Creating Satisfied Customers That Do the Selling For You
- Sales Rich – If You Are in Business Then You Are in Sales
- Team Rich – Transform your Team into a Championship Team

And many more…

TESTIMONIALS

"Milton is an incredibly experienced businessperson from the real world, here in Melbourne and regional Victoria. We wanted to adapt and evolve our business and needed guidance from someone with the right skillset and cultural fit. From our first meeting, we knew Milton was the right person for the job and we embarked on our journey covering key areas such as accounting, leadership, sales, marketing, customer service, production and human resource management. Milton's professionalism, maturity and wisdom combined with his sense of humour and zest for life gave us the boost we needed. We now understand our business better than ever and the return on investment speaks for itself. We can highly recommend Milton to help achieve your business goals and empower you to succeed."

– **Megan Corbett** (Owner, Wood Wizards Kitchens)

"From our first meeting I really resonated with Milton's business experience and how he understood our company; he could clearly see what we had been missing and how we could improve. With his support, enthusiasm, fantastic eye for detail and wonderful sense of humour, our business has moved closer to the level it needs to be. We have only just begun in the past 2.5 months, however, we have had an enormous amount of improvement in customer service, team management and financial cash-flow, and we cannot wait to see the further results of Milton's coaching. Most importantly, I found Milton to really understand me and listen to where I wanted my business to go. Once you find the right business coach, even for an already successful business, the improvements and growth are incomparable."
– **Georgie Webster** (Owner, Bonlex Australia)

"I was lucky to participate in a workshop designed and facilitated by Milton at a time when businesses were experiencing unprecedented pressures due to Covid-19. I was never quite sure of what I would gain from a 3-hour workshop particularly when the problems appeared almost insurmountable. However, I can honestly say that Milton provided some grounded advice, amazing encouragement, and practical business strategies that I can definitely use to move forward. Highly worthwhile."
– **Jackie Goodyear** (Owner, Jeds)

"Milton Collins has been a crucial mentor in the development of our process, structure and accountability within the business. He has high attention for detail and is a results-driven coach who has provided unwavering support not only to myself but the whole team. The process has provided clarity around our goals, structure around our processes but most importantly unity within a culture. I

highly recommend Milton. He is genuinely interested in ensuring positive results and has a wealth of experience to back it up. He can be tough but that's what you want when you are aiming to be the best you can be."
– **Debra Lawry** (Director, Ray White Romsey)

"We had a year of coaching with Milton after meeting him at a public talk. It was a good opportunity to reflect on our current systems and implement positive change. After years in practice, our eyes were unaccustomed to seeing areas for improvement. Coaching helped us take a step back, review our processes and shake things up."
– **Tiffani Clingin** (Social Worker, Liberty Health and Happiness)

"Milton is no stranger to business, with a proven record of delivering exceptional results in all areas of business. He possesses an intuitive capacity to identify key drivers and successfully implement plans and strategies, leading many businesses to sustained success."
– **Derek Jones** (Currie Communications)

"Milton has a wealth of experience and is extremely professional, and he has helped my business grow beyond expectation in the last few months. I highly recommend Milton at Action Coach."
– **Micheal Nalesnyik** (Mortgage Broker, Loan Market)

"Milton is a highly regarded business coach who applies his extensive experience to help businesses grow. Highly recommended if you're looking to grow your business sustainably and with confidence."
– **Will Smith** (Business Owner, Macedon Digital)

"Milton is very knowledgeable, experienced, directed and results-based geared towards performance. Definitely recommended."
– **Chaz Arachchi** (Founder, Robusq Group)

"I am a previous client of Milton Collins who was an amazing coach to our organisation helping us from 2 clients to 500 in one year. His input was amazing."
– **Cristina Karvonidis** (General Manager, Give a Care)

ACKNOWLEDGEMENTS

I would like to thank the following people and organisations.

The ActionCOACH® community led by founder Brad Sugars, and the amazingly supportive and generous league of Business Coaches. I was welcomed into the fold immediately and made to feel part of the worldwide team. The sharing of knowledge, experience and expertise is second to none and continues to excel and grow. So much of this book is the essence of ActionCOACH® and the result of my learnings and past experiences.

The Dean Publishing team led by Susan Dean and supported by her family who have become friends. The whole Dean Publishing team are talented, hardworking and professional, they provide such a depth of support that goes far beyond what could be expected from a publishing company. This is especially driven by the fabulous Natalie Deane, my editor, that did far more than edit. Her research, encouragement, inspiration and discipline made this book happen.

My incredible daughter Emma, who has worked closely with me both in business and on the final stages of this book. Her skill and ability far exceeds her years and the rate that she produces quality work from marketing to admin, to graphics and speech writing, never ceases to amaze. I have been very fortunate to have her working with me until she now pursues her own career in which I have no doubt that she will excel.

The loyal support of my current and past clients in all my businesses — all have given me so much pleasure and taught me so much in return. I have been very fortunate to be involved in so many lives and businesses.

To my colleagues and team members over the years — thank you for your support and for teaching me the importance of staying connected in both good and tough times. Thank you for allowing me to work on leadership and team development whilst making many mistakes along the way, but to also grow and achieve great things.

And finally, to my friends — both old and new — you have always stood by me even during some of my most challenging times. The laughter, the fun, the outrageous times and the serious conversations, I am more than fortunate to have so many true friends. Thank you.

ENDNOTES

1   Vernon, R. J., Sutherland, C. A., Young, A. W., & Hartley, T. (2014). 'Modeling first impressions from highly variable facial images', *Proceedings of the National Academy of Sciences of the United States of America*, 111(32), E3353–E3361. https://doi.org/10.1073/pnas.1409860111

2   G. Gunaydin, E. Selcuk, V. Zayas. (2016) 'Impressions Based on a Portrait Predict, 1-Month Later, Impressions Following a Live Interaction'. *Social Psychological and Personality Science*, DOI: 10.1177/1948550616662123
    Cornell University. (November 28 2016) 'When judging other people, first impressions last', *ScienceDaily*. Retrieved April 7, 2021 www.sciencedaily.com/releases/2016/11/161128171723.htm

3   McAleer P, Todorov A, Belin P (2014) 'How Do You Say 'Hello'? Personality Impressions from Brief Novel Voices'. *PLoS ONE* 9(3): e90779. https://doi.org/10.1371/journal.pone.0090779

4   Ibid.

5   Carmody, D. P., & Lewis, M. (2006) 'Brain activation when hearing one's own and others' names', *Brain research*, 1116(1), 153-158. https://doi.org/10.1016/j.brainres.2006.07.121

6   Genesys Global Survey (November 2009) *The Cost of Poor Customer Service: The Economic Impact of the Customer Experience and Engagement in 16 Key Economies*, Genesys. http://www. ancoralearning.com.au/wp-content/uploads/2014/07/Genesys_ Global_Survey09_screen.pdf

7   Ibid.

8   "Serial Switchers" (2018) report. Previously published under New Voice Media (Now Vonage®). www.vonage.com.au

9   Genesys, Global Survey (November 2009) *The Cost of Poor Customer Service: The Economic Impact of the Customer Experience and Engagement in 16 Key Economies*, Genesys. http://www. ancoralearning.com.au/wp-content/uploads/2014/07/Genesys_ Global_Survey09_screen.pdf

10 "Serial Switchers" (2018) report. Previously published under New Voice Media (Now Vonage®). www.vonage.com.au

11 *The New imperial encyclopedia and dictionary* (1906) San Francisco, Pacific Newspaper Union. Sourced online: https://archive.org/ details/newimperialencyc11unse

12 12. Dfarhud, D., Malmir, M., & Khanahmadi, M. (2014) 'Happiness & Health: The Biological Factors- Systematic Review Article', *Iranian journal of public health*, 43(11), 1468–1477.

13 zappos.com

14 Berns, G. S., McClure, S. M., Pagnoni, G., & Montague, P. R. (2001) 'Predictability modulates human brain response to reward', *The Journal of neuroscience : the official journal of the Society for Neuroscience*, 21(8), 2793–2798. https://doi.org/10.1523/ JNEUROSCI.21-08-02793.2001

15 Sommerfeld, Julia. (n.d) 'Human brain gets a kick out of surprises', Emory College and MSNBC 'Publicity'. http://www.ccnl.emory.edu/ Publicity/MSNBC.HTM

16 *Cambridge Dictionary*, accessed online April 12 2021, https:// dictionary.cambridge.org/dictionary/english/corporate-culture

17 J.Gold Associates, LLC. (August 2018)' Older PCs in SMB Cost Study Selected Results,', A J. Gold Associates Research Report. http://www.jgoldassociates.com Used with permission from Jack. E. Gold

18 Branson, Richard. (August 31, 2015) 'You Can't Fake Personality, Passion or Purpose', LinkedIn article published by Virgin Group. https://www.linkedin.com/pulse/how-i-hire-you-cant-fake-personality-passion-purpose-richard-branson

19 Jeff Bezos Quotes. (n.d.). BrainyQuote.com. Retrieved April 11, 2021, from BrainyQuote.com Web site: https://www.brainyquote.com/quotes/jeff_bezos_450020

20 A_Z Quotes, 'Customer Loyalty Quotes'. Retrieved April 11 2021. https://www.azquotes.com/quotes/topics/customer-loyalty.html

21 Gracious Quotes (September 14 2020) 'Top 53 Jeff Bezos Quotes on Success (AMAZON)' https://graciousquotes.com/jeff-bezos

22 Todorov, Georgie, (March 11 2021) '66 Ridiculously Useful Email Marketing Statistics Every Marketer Needs to Know', Semrush, https://www.semrush.com/blog/email-marketing-stats

23 Australian Bureau of Statistics, (30-09-2020) 'General Social Survey: Summary Results, Australia.' https://www.abs.gov.au/statistics/people/people-and-communities/general-social-survey-summary-results-australia/latest-release#data-download

24 Pennebaker, James & Chung, Cindy. (2007). Expressive Writing, Emotional Upheavals, and Health.
Kacewicz, Ewa & Slatcher, Richard & Pennebaker, James. (2006). 'Expressive Writing: An Alternative to Traditional Methods', 10.1007/0-387-36899-X_13.

25 24. Di Stefano, Giada and Gino, Francesca and Pisano, Gary and Staats, Bradley R., (June 14, 2016). 'Making Experience Count: The Role of Reflection in Individual Learning' Harvard Business School NOM Unit Working Paper No. 14-093, Harvard Business School Technology & Operations Mgt. Unit Working Paper No. 14-093, HEC Paris Research Paper No. SPE-2016-1181, Available

at SSRN: https://ssrn.com/abstract=2414478 or http://dx.doi. org/10.2139/ssrn.2414478

26 Jonker, L, Elferink-Gemser, MT, de Roos, IM & Visscher, C (2012) 'The Role of Reflection in Sport Expertise', *Sport psychologist*, vol. 26, no. 2, pp. 224-242.

27 Lepore, Stephen. (1997) 'Expressive writing moderates the relation between intrusive thoughts and depressive symptoms', *Journal of personality and social psychology*. 73. 1030-7. 10.1037//0022-3514.73.5.1030.
Klein, K., & Boals, A. (2001) 'Expressive writing can increase working memory capacity', *Journal of experimental psychology*. General, 130(3), 520-533. https://doi.org/10.1037//0096-3445.130.3.520

28 Scullin, M. K., Krueger, M. L., Ballard, H. K., Pruett, N., & Bliwise, D. L. (2018) 'The effects of bedtime writing on difficulty falling asleep: A polysomnographic study comparing to-do lists and completed activity lists', *Journal of experimental psychology. General, 147*(1), 139–146. https://doi.org/10.1037/xge0000374

29 Waitzkin, Josh. (2008) *The art of learning : an inner journey to optimal performance*. New York, Free Press. https://www.joshwaitzkin.com

30 McLeod, Colin. 'Why are Australian stat-ups failing?' *Pursuit*. University of Melbourne. https://pursuit.unimelb.edu.au/articles/why-are-australian-start-ups-failing

31 Australian Centre for Business Growth (20 November 2018) 'New studies reveal why Australian SMEs fail'. University of South Australia's Business School (2014 — 2018). Image and statistics used with permission. https://www.unisa.edu.au/Media-Centre/Releases/2018/new-study-reveals-why-australian-smes-fail

32 Cross, Rob; Grant, Adam; Rebele, Reb. 'Collaborative Overload', *Harvard Business Review*, https://hbr.org/2016/01/collaborative-overload [originally published in *HBR Magazine* January-February 2016]. https://hbr.org/2016/01/collaborative-overload

33 E. T. Klemmer, F. W. Snyder, 'Measurement of Time Spent Communicating', *Journal of Communication*, Volume 22, Issue 2, June 1972, Pages 142-158, https://doi.org/10.1111/j.1460-2466.1972. tb00141.x

34 Gallup, State of the Global Workplace — Gallup Report (2017) https://www.gallup.com/workplace/257552/state-global-workplace-2017.aspx

35 Ibid.

36 https://claytonchristensen.com

37 Ibid.

38 Wu, Lingfei & Wang, Dashun & Evans, James. (2019) 'Large teams develop and small teams disrupt science and technology'. *Nature*. 566. 1. 10.1038/s41586-019-0941-9

39 Flade, Peter, Asplund, Jim, Elliot, Gwen (9 October 8, 2015) Workplace. 'Employees Who Use Their Strengths Outperform Those Who Don't.' Gallup.com. https://www.gallup.com/workplace/236561/ employees-strengths-outperform-don.aspx

40 Ibid.

41 Sugars, Brad. (April 20, 2016) '6 Keys to a Winning Team' , ActionCOACH.com https://www.actioncoach.com/blog/6-keys-to-a-winning-team

42 BNI® — CEO Corner, (February 7 2017) 'What Makes a Strong Business Leader?' https://www.bni.com/the-latest/blog-news/what-makes-a-strong-business-leader

43 Workboard. Published infographic online. https://www.workboard.com//infographic-set-achieve-goals

44 McKinsey & Company (2010) Global Survey: Innovation and commercialization, McKinsey Global Survey results.

45 Groysberg, Boris, and Connolly, Katherine. (September 2013) 'Great Leaders Who Make the Mix Work', *Harvard Business Review* 91, no. 968-76. https://www.hbs.edu/faculty/Pages/item.aspx?num=45425

46 Ibid.

47 Branson, Richard. (1998) *Losing my virginity: the autobiography.* London, Virgin Pub.

48 Housman, Michael, and Dylan Minor. 'Toxic Workers.' Harvard Business School Working Paper, No. 16-057, October 2015. (Revised November 2015.)

49 Australian Bureau of Statistics (ABS) monthly Labour Force Survey and Participation, Job Search and Mobility, Australia (PJSM) survey conducted throughout Australia in February 2019.

50 Keller, Scott; Meaney, Mary. McKinsey & Company, (June 28, 2017) McKinsey Quarterly, 'High-performing teams: a timeless leadership topic', https://www.mckinsey.com/business-functions/organization/our-insights/high-performing-teams-a-timeless-leadership-topic

51 53. Julian F Thayer, Bart Verkuil, Jos F Brosschotj, Kampschroer Kevin, Anthony West, Carolyn Sterling, Israel C Christie, Darrell R Abernethy, John J Sollers, Giovanni Cizza, Andrea H Marques, Esther M Sternberg (1 August 2010) 'Effects of the physical work environment on physiological measures of stress', *European journal of cardiovascular prevention and rehabilitation*, Volume 17, Issue 4, , Pages 431- 439, https://doi.org/10.1097/HJR.0b013e328336923a

52 Ruggeri, Amanda. U.S. News (Oct 22 2019) 'Jim Sinegal: Costco CEO Focuses on Employees' Usnews.com. https://www.usnews.com/news/best-leaders/articles/2009/10/22/jim-sinegal-costco-ceo-focuses-on-employees

53 Ibid.

54 Gerdeman, Dina. (28 January 2019) 'Forget Cash. Here are Better Ways To Motivate Employees' , Harvard Business School. https://hbswk.hbs.edu/item/forget-cash-here-are-better-ways-to-motivate-employees

55 Strack Rainer, von der Linden, Carsten, Booker, Mike, Strohmayr. Andrea. (October 6 2014) 'Decoding Global Talent', Boston Consulting Group, Bcg.com https://www.bcg.com/en-au/

publications/2014/people-organization-human-resources-decoding-global-talent

56 Kaufman, T., Christensen, D.T. and Newton, A. (2015) 'Employee Performance: What Causes Great Work?' National Research by Cicero Group. Commissioned by the O. C. Tanner Institute.

57 Barbe, Walter Burke; Swassing, Raymond H.; Milone, Michael N. (1979). *Teaching through modality strengths: concepts practices.* Columbus, Ohio: Zaner-Bloser.

58 Roell, Kelly (Aug. 26, 2020) 'Understanding Visual, Auditory, and Kinesthetic Learning Styles.' ThoughtCo, thoughtco.com/three-different-learning-styles-3212040.

59 The Marketing Study Guide (n.d.) [online] Accessed May 28, 2021. https://www.marketingstudyguide.com/examples-brand-touchpoints-apple

60 Zaltman, Gerald. (2003) *How Consumers Think : Essential Insights into the Mind of the Market* / G. Zaltman.

61 RYBACK, D. (1998). *Putting emotional intelligence to work: successful leadership is more than IQ.* Boston, Butterworth-Heinemann. http://public.eblib.com/choice/publicfullrecord.aspx?p=1024589.

62 Caruso, D. R., Mayer, J. D., & Salovey, P. (2002) 'Relation of an ability measure of emotional intelligence to personality', *Journal of personality assessment, 79*(2), 306–320. https://doi.org/10.1207/S15327752JPA7902_12

63 Ibid.

64 National Association of Colleges and Employers (July 13 2020) 'Job Outlook 2020' (https://www.naceweb.org) https://www.naceweb.org/talent-acquisition/candidate-selection/key-attributes-employers-want-to-see-on-students-resumes

65 Harrell, Melissa; Barbato, Lauren. Rework. (February 27 2018) 'Great managers still matter: the evolution of Google's Project Oxygen' https://rework.withgoogle.com/blog/the-evolution-of-project-oxygen

66 Lambert, Fred. Electrek [blog post] (Jun 2nd 2017) 'Elon Musk says he will perform same tasks as Tesla workers getting injured in the factory.' https://electrek.co/2017/06/02/elon-musk-tesla-injury-factory

67 Caruso, D.R., Mayer, J.D. & Salovey, P. (2002) 'Relation of an ability measure of emotional intelligence to personality', *Journal of Personality Assessment*, 79(2), 306-320. DOI 10.1.1.584.9650 Munro, M., Munro, A., Lemmer, K. & Pretorius, M. (2015) 'Theatre strategies to develop emotional intelligence skills in business communication: An exploratory study', *Southern African Business Review* 19(2), 1-26. DOI: 10.25159/1998-8125/5838

68 Wilcox, Laura. (7th July, 2017) Professional Development Blog — 'Emotional Intelligence Is No Soft Skill.' Harvard Extension School.

69 Goleman, Daniel. (January 2004) Emotional Intelligence.: 'What Makes A Leader', *Harvard Business Review*.

70 Bradberry, T., & Greaves, J. (2009) *Emotional intelligence 2.0*. San Diego, California: TalentSmart® https://www.talentsmarteq.com/about-eq

71 http://www.danielgoleman.info

72 Malti, T., Ongley, S.F., Peplak, J., Chaparro, M.P., Buchmann, M., Zuffianò, A., & Cui, L. (2016) 'Children's Sympathy, Guilt, and Moral Reasoning in Helping, Cooperation, and Sharing: A 6-Year Longitudinal Study'. *Child development*, 87 6, 1783-1795.

73 Maia Szalavitz and Bruce Perry (1 April 2011) *Born for Love: Why Empathy is Essential - and Endangered*. HarperCollins - US; Reprint edition.

74 Konrath, S. H., O'Brien, E. H., & Hsing, C. (2011) 'Changes in Dispositional Empathy in American College Students Over Time: A Meta-Analysis'. *Personality and Social Psychology Review*, 15(2), 180–198. https://doi.org/10.1177/1088868310377395

75 https://micheleborba.com

76 Rivera, Alejandra. (26 August 2019) 'Is empathy good for business?' The University of Melbourne, *Pursuit*. First published on in Inside

Business. https://pursuit.unimelb.edu.au/articles/is-empathy-good-for-business

77 Ibid.

78 Ibid.

79 World Economic Forum, (1–2 June 2016)Human Capital Outlook Association of Southeast Asian Nations (ASEAN), Kuala Lumpur, Malaysia.

80 Guest, D. (September 17, 1991) 'The hunt is on for the Renaissance Man of Computing', *The Independent* (London). Retreived from: Baratta, Daniele. (2017) 'The "T" shaped designer expertise. The "reverse-T" shaped designer horizon', *The Design Journal*. 20. S4784-S4786. 10.1080/14606925.2017.1352992.

81 Hamdi, Shabnam & Silong, Abu & Omar, Zoharah & Mohd Rasdi, Roziah & Nisar, Tahir. (2016) 'Impact of T-shaped skill and top management support on innovation speed; the moderating role of technology uncertainty'. *Cogent Business & Management*. 3. 1153768. 10.1080/23311975.2016.1153768.

82 Ashley Friedlein, (November 8, 2012) Marketing Week article: "Why modern marketers need to be pi-people", (Econsultancy.com) Permission from centaurmedia.com. https://www.marketingweek.com/why-modern-marketers-need-to-be-pi-people

83 Sharma, Gaurav (May 7, 2018) 'Which Letter-shaped employee you are?' LinkedIn article. https://www.linkedin.com/pulse/which-letter-shaped-employee-you-gaurav-sharma

84 Teodoridis, F., Bikard, M., & Vakili, K. (2019) 'Creativity at the Knowledge Frontier: The Impact of Specialization in Fast- and Slow-paced Domains', *Administrative Science Quarterly*, 64(4), 894–927. https://doi.org/10.1177/0001839218793384

85 Ibid.

86 Amazon (July 11, 2019) Press release: 'Amazon Pledges to Upskill 100,000 U.S. Employees for In-Demand Jobs by 2025'. https://press.aboutamazon.com/news-releases/news-release-details/amazon-pledges-upskill-100000-us-employees-demand-jobs-2025

87 Ibid.

88 Cleveland, Marisa & Cleveland, Simon. (2018) Building Engaged Communities—A Collaborative Leadership Approach. Smart Cities. 1. 155-162. 10.3390/smartcities1010009
Corrigan, Dean. (2009) 'The Changing Role of Schools and Higher Education Institutions With Respect to Community-Based Interagency Collaboration and Interprofessional Partnerships', *Peabody Journal of Education*. 75. 176-195. 10.1207/S15327930PJE7503_12.

89 Quotesia.'Bill Gates quotes', https://quotesia.com/bill-gates-quotes

90 Australian Government. (2016) *Australian Small Business and Family Enterprise Ombudsman | Small Business in the Australian Economy.* https://www.asbfeo.gov.au/sites/default/files/Small_Business_Statistical_Report-Final.pdf

www.ingramcontent.com/pod-product-compliance
Lightning Source LLC
Chambersburg PA
CBHW071200210326
41597CB00016B/1614